S0-ADM-632

SEA-CAPTAINS' HOUSES AND ROSE-COVERED COTTAGES

SEA-CAPTAINS' HOUSES
and ROSE-COVERED COTTAGES
The Architectural Heritage of Nantucket Island

Margaret Moore Booker, Rose Gonnella, *and* Patricia Egan Butler
Principal Photography by Jordi Cabré

UNIVERSE PUBLISHING
in association with THE EGAN INSTITUTE OF MARITIME STUDIES,
NANTUCKET, MASSACHUSETTS

The publishers gratefully acknowledge the support of Furthermore: a program of the J.M. Kaplan Fund.

All photographs are by Jordi Cabré unless otherwise indicated.
FRONT COVER: *105 Main Street, Built ca. 1690–1757 for Christopher Starbuck.*
BACK COVER: *Rose-Covered Cottage with Porthole Window, 'Sconset.*
PAGE ii: *Rose-Covered Cottage, 'Sconset.*

First published in the United States of America in 2003
by UNIVERSE PUBLISHING
A Division of Rizzoli International Publications, Inc.
300 Park Avenue South
New York, NY 10010
www.rizzoliusa.com

© 2003 by Margaret Moore Booker, Rose Gonnella, and Patricia Egan Butler

All rights reserved. No part of this publication may be reproduced, stored in
a retrieval system, or transmitted in any form or by any means, electronic, mechanical,
photocopying, recording, or otherwise, without prior consent of the publishers.

2003 2004 2005 2006 2007 / 10 9 8 7 6 5 4 3 2 1

Printed in the United States of America
Design by Sara E. Stemen

ISBN: 0-7893-0880-0

LIBRARY OF CONGRESS CATALOGING-IN-PUBLICATION DATA
Booker, Margaret Moore.
    Sea-captains' houses and rose-covered cottages : the architectural heritage of Nantucket Island / Margaret Moore
    Booker, Rose Gonnella, and Patricia Egan Butler ; photographs by Jordi Cabré.—1st ed.
        p. cm.
    Includes bibliographical references and index.
    ISBN 0-7893-0880-0 (hardcover : alk. paper)
    1. Architecture, Domestic—Massachusetts—Nantucket Island. 2. Nantucket Island (Mass.)—Buildings, structures,
    etc. I. Gonnella, Rose. II. Butler, Patricia Egan. III. Title.
    NA7235.M42N363 2003
    728'.37'0974497—DC21
                                         2003009024

Monument Grocery, Built 1875, 106 Main Street, ca. 1880.
Building demolished, facade dismantled August 2001.
Photograph Courtesy of the Nantucket Historical Association.

To the memory of 106 Main Street

and

to all those dedicated to preserving Nantucket's architectural heritage

Contents

Foreword

O_{NE} of my most memorable days was my introduction to Nantucket in 1965. A friend asked me to accompany him across the island on horseback. For most of the day we rode over the rolling heathlands and moors in the middle of the island, punctuated by scrub oaks, shade, and tupelo trees. The landscape stretched languidly before us, with the occasional long vista to the glimmering sea, as we climbed the low, sandy hills.

As we made our way to Eel Point at the northwest corner of the island, where we galloped along the shifting sands of the barrier beach, we were caught up in a magical spell of timelessness. Riding through the woody, flowering landscape of blue-eyed grass, rosa rugosa, bayberry, and beach plum, as colors filtered from deep blue to soft pinks and grays, we saw little evidence of the modern hand. During that day, we stopped only twice to open gates, an almost uninterrupted ride across the very heart of the island.

This, to me, is still the essence of Nantucket. Almost forty years later, it is still a precarious balance of land, sea, and buildings, shifting planes of light and color. Although the passage of time has brought more visitors, traffic, and structures to this island, the essential quality remains untouched. The rush of the tide and sweep of the sky on this beautiful island are as much a part of the lives of contemporary island dwellers as they were for the original settlers.

Our greatest challenge today is to preserve Nantucket's sense of place so that it can be passed on to future generations. As this book illustrates, whether it is a simple shingle lean-to, brick Federal-style mansion, clapboard Victorian summer cottage, or a modern home based on past traditions, architecture plays an integral role in the island's unique identity. The built environment and fragile landscape are interwoven in a harmonious way on Nantucket, and both need our protection.

—*Graham Gund, February 2003*

{ OPPOSITE }
Aerial View of
Nantucket Island.
Photograph by Robert Morrison.

Introduction

Margaret Moore Booker

*O*NE late-nineteenth-century writer suggested that Nantucket was a "quaint old place" with "odd-looking specimens of architecture" that are "shingled, shangled, shongled, and shungled."[1] Indeed, today, upon first stepping onto the sandy shores of this island, which lies twenty-four miles off the south coast of Cape Cod, Massachusetts (FIGURE 1), one might gain the impression that all of the buildings are, and always have been, covered in weathered gray shingles, and are of simple construction. In fact Nantucket's architecture was once sheathed in a variety of rich colors (FIGURE 2). As the aforementioned writer noted, "in years gone by [these shingled houses] were painted red, green, or yellow." There is also abundant evidence that the island was, and continues to be, home to a wide range of architectural styles, from the stark lean-to and typical Nantucket house, to the balanced classical Federal and Greek Revival, to the eclectic Victorian, to the streamlined modern.

Nantucket Island, a fifteen-mile-long and three-mile-wide "elbow of sand," as Herman Melville called it in *Moby Dick*, is one of America's national treasures. Consisting of acres of rolling heathland, small ponds, and wide expanses of unspoiled beaches, the island is home to several small villages containing one of the largest and most important collections of historic buildings in the United States. An astounding 2,400 historic structures, including eight hundred pre-Civil War buildings, are still extant on the island today and represent the character and charm of Nantucket's people and their glorious past.[2]

While there are preservation-minded individuals and organizations on the island, including the Historic District Commission, Nantucket Preservation Alliance, and Nantucket Preservation Trust, as well as preservation regulations, there is still a widespread need for educating the public on the merits of Nantucket's important historic architecture, and the necessity of preserving it for future generations. Our primary goal in writing this book is an attempt to meet both these needs, as well as to celebrate the architectural gems on the island and to preserve in print buildings that some day may be altered or demolished.

{ OPPOSITE }
View of Nantucket Town and Unitarian Church Tower from Summer Street.
Photograph by Gregory Spaid.

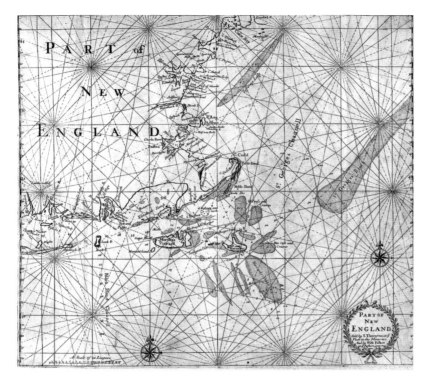

FIGURE 1: Map of Part of New England, 1698. *Engraving published by John Thornton and William Fisher for* The English Pilot, The Fourth Book *(London, second edition, 1698).* Photograph Courtesy Peabody Essex Museum.

FIGURE 2: Phebe Folger, A Perspective View of Part of the Town of Nantucket, Taken from an East Window in the House of Walter Folger, 1797. Watercolor on paper. *This scene was drawn by Quaker schoolmistress Phebe Folger (1771–1857) from the window of her brother's house at 8 Pleasant Street. The red houses she portrayed are proof of the fact that the "Gray Lady"—as Nantucket, with its predominantly gray-shingled houses, has so often been called over the centuries—was not always as gray as was once believed. This and another drawing by Folger (Chapter 2, figure 25) are the two earliest views of Nantucket Town that exist today.* FMS Typ 245, Department of Printing and Graphic Arts, Houghton Library, Harvard College Library.

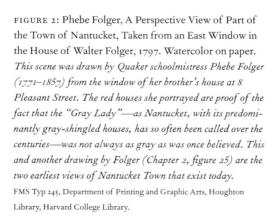

{ LEFT }

FIGURE 3: 19 Hussey, Built for Timothy Barnard, 1758. Illustration by Rose Gonnella, 1995. *This is a classic early lean-to house, one of three on Hussey Street, in Nantucket Town.*

{ RIGHT }

FIGURE 4: 8 Mill Street, 1922. *Built in the last quarter of the eighteenth century, this "typical Nantucket house" has a proliferation of "warts" and ells jutting off the side and rear of the building, which were added in later years.* Courtesy of the Nantucket Historical Association.

Several centuries of social, cultural, religious, and economic narratives are embodied in Nantucket's architectural landscape. The story begins with the island's first inhabitants—Native Americans—who lived off the abundant resources of the land and sea and fashioned their rustic homes out of bent saplings covered with grass mats. In 1659 English settlers arrived and built simple homes with steep gabled roofs that reflected the traditions of their homeland. They settled at Capaum Harbor on the north shore. As the island's first families grew and needed more living space, a lean-to was typically added to the rear of the house (FIGURE 3).

When the Religious Society of Friends, the Quakers, gained a stronghold on the island in the early 1700s, the group adhered to a Zen-like quality of restraint, fashioning homes distinguished by their simplicity, superb carpentry, and beautiful proportions. Many of the builders of these early homes were also shipwrights, and their houses reflect the influence of shipbuilding in the streamlined tightness of the plan, excellent craftsmanship, and architectural details such as porthole windows, rope handrails, and roof walks. These features are particularly noticeable in the "typical Nantucket house" (FIGURE 4) and in the small fishermen's cottages in Siasconset, on the eastern shore of the island.

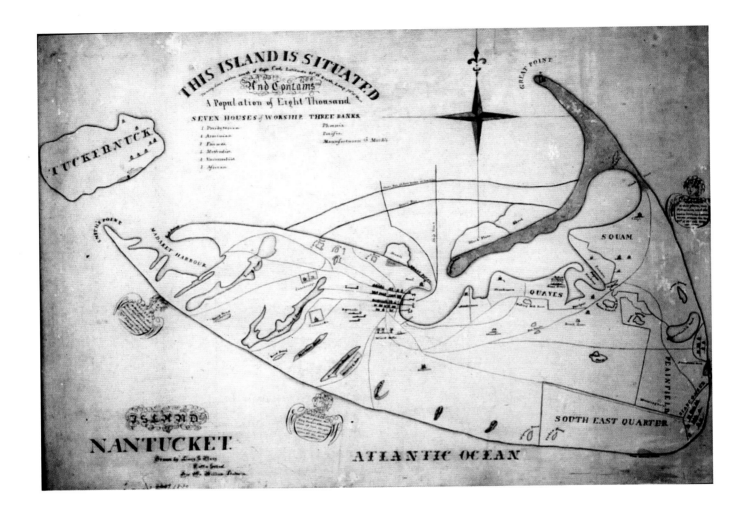

FIGURE 5: Lucy S. Macy, Map of Nantucket, ca. 1829. Watercolor and ink on paper. *Made at the Coffin School by student Lucy Macy (1812–1875), this map gives a fairly accurate indication of the overall shape of the island and the populated areas. In a simple, naive manner Macy drew tiny images of important structures—including the windmills, ropewalks (where rope was manufactured), lighthouses, and some homes in the settlements of Nantucket Town, Siasconset, and elsewhere around the island.* Courtesy of the Nantucket Historical Association.

FIGURE 6: Henry C. Platt, View of Nantucket from the Harbor in 1833, ca. 1883. Pen and ink on paper. *This rendering gives a good representation of the bustling, crowded Nantucket Town and harbor during the height of the whaling era. Henry "Harry" Platt (1850–1895), was an artist, photographer, and art teacher who began visiting the island in the 1880s, and eventually established a studio in Nantucket Town.* Courtesy of the Nantucket Historical Association.

In 1690 the English began the practice of "alongshore whaling," killing right whales from small open boats, and in 1712 they began specializing in hunting sperm whales, which took whalemen as far north as the arctic circle and as far south as the Falkland Islands. Soon after the Revolutionary War, huge reserves of sperm whales were discovered in the Pacific and by 1792, Nantucketers commanded thirty-three of the thirty-nine whaleships there.

As writer Joseph Sansom noted, by 1811 the town (by then moved from Capaum Harbor to its present location) had a thriving population, with new streets laid out in straight lines and a number of new houses built with extravagantly high ceilings. However, despite the activity of a flourishing seaport, Sansom commented, "Everything here reminds one of a religious community…the tranquility of a convent pervades the streets."[3]

After the War of 1812, when America gained economic freedom from the British and national pride was soaring, Nantucket's whaling industry reached a zenith of prosperity and the Quakers no longer had a stronghold on the community. In the 1820s and 1830s, with a population of almost ten thousand inhabitants, and property valued at six million dollars, the island was a thriving commercial center and the third largest port in New England (FIGURE 5). Ships crowded the harbor and the town was bustling with whaling-related industries, including seventeen factories, nineteen candle manufacturers, ten ropewalks, and twenty-two cooperages (barrel-making shops), which employed hundreds of people and created an air of prosperity (FIGURE 6).

Nantucketers built up immense fortunes and used them to transform the downtown into a small but elegant and modern port town, complete with elm-lined streets, brick commercial buildings, and stately homes (FIGURE 7). Most of the mansions were built on cobblestoned Main Street, which flows through the heart of town to the harbor. Architectural historian Vincent Scully aptly described these blocks of homes as "fine, flat-fronted or columned mansions of the Starbucks and other shipowners and whaling captains [that stand] close to each other and to the cobbled pavement. Dappled in sunlight,

{ OPPOSITE }

FIGURE 7: Main Street Mansion, Built (or remodeled) ca. 1830s. *Still paved with cobblestones and lined with mansions built with whale oil money, Main Street retains much of its original character today. This house has both classical and Gothic Revival elements; an example of the latter is visible in the pointed arch window in the pediment.*

{ ABOVE LEFT }

FIGURE 8: Moors' End, 19 Pleasant Street, Built in 1829–34 for Jared Coffin (1784–1860). *A good example of the early Federal style, Moors' End was the first all-brick house built on the island and is notable for its beautiful semicircular "blind fan" rising over the doorway. Like many others who made their fortune in the whaling industry, Jared Coffin built a large edifice that is a bold statement of his wealth, power, and ambition.*

{ ABOVE RIGHT }

FIGURE 9: William Hadwen Mansion, Built in 1844, at 96 Main Street. *The height of the Greek Revival style is realized in this house, which is distinguished by its Greek temple facade with the large pediment and Ionic columns. Built by prolific island builder Frederick Brown Coleman, it was the home of magnate William Hadwen (1791–1862), one of the island's wealthiest men and largest manufacturer of whale oil and spermaceti candles. It is now owned by the Nantucket Historical Association.* Courtesy of the Nantucket Historical Association.

{ LEFT }

FIGURE 10: 82 Main Street, at Corner of Ray's Court, Built in Early 19th Century. *This five-bay Federal-style home has two architectural features that are often associated with Nantucket houses: a roof "walk" (a platform enclosed by a hand railing and originally intended to provide easy access to the roof in event of a chimney fire) and double-sided stairs.* Photograph by Gregory Spaid.

{ BELOW }

FIGURE 11: Main Street Before the Great Fire, ca. Early 1840s. *The Pacific Bank and Methodist Church at the top of Main Street are the only buildings in this earliest known view of Nantucket Town that survived the Great Fire of 1846, and remain extant today. The wooden homes and businesses on the right side of the photograph were, not surprisingly, replaced with brick buildings after the fire.* Courtesy of the Nantucket Historical Association.

FIGURE 12: Old North Wharf, Nantucket Island. *After the decline of the whaling industry, the island suffered a series of economic blows, and the waterfront and town took on a seedy, desolate appearance.* Courtesy of the Nantucket Historical Association.

these blocks seem hardly to belong to the United States but to an island jewel, like the Calypso's in the heart of the ocean. Here the captains slept uneasily, heads starting up with grate of iron on cobbles, accustomed as they were, as Melville tells us, to pillow on the lucid rush of porpoises and whales."[4]

When building their mansions, the newly rich and style-conscious island merchants embraced the current vogue for classic forms, including the Federal style (FIGURE 8), distinguished by doorways with slender columns and fanlight windows, and the Greek Revival style (FIGURE 9), recognizable by the pediment and columns that echo the classical Greek temple. After visiting the island one journalist observed that these new buildings were "neat, clean, and orderly, 'blazing away' in white paint, [with] all the majesty of Greek design and ornament ... exhibiting on the part of owners and occupants a *desire* to have everything about them in the best possible taste."[5]

In the mid-1840s, Nantucket's whaling industry began its precipitous decline. Many factors contributed to this, including the Great Fire of July 13, 1846, which began in a hat factory on the south side of Main Street and eventually consumed one third of the town (FIGURE 11). Although it was quickly rebuilt, Nantucket could no longer compete with the rival whaling port of New Bedford. In addition to having a deep-water harbor unencumbered with shoals, New Bedford enjoyed the benefit of direct access to the nation's burgeoning railroad system. With the discovery of gold in California, Nantucket lost a quarter of its voting population to the goldfields in nine months.

After the demise of the whaling industry in the mid-1840s, the island experienced a series of economic blows, and for some thirty years, few buildings were erected or altered. One visitor commented that in 1847 the town was "composed mainly of old weather-beaten frame houses covered with pine shingles, and entirely destitute of all architectural graces or the embellishment of paint; the streets are crooked and straggling, and so sandy that you have to wade through them, rather than walk."[6]

As the island experienced a period of economic decline from the mid-1850s throughout much of the 1860s, the population greatly decreased and many island homes were abandoned, waiting for new fortunes to bring them back to life (FIGURE 12). This financial depression led to the forced "preservation" of many early structures, and is why Nantucket has one of the largest caches of pre–Civil War homes in the United States.

During the mid-nineteenth-century depression years, some early houses were taken down and removed to other places, both on and off the island. The moving of houses (FIGURE 13), which began with the transfer of homes from the settlement at Capaum Harbor to Sherburne (now Nantucket Town) in the late 1700s, is a tradition that is carried on to this day. By the time the English settlers arrived, the island was largely devoid of trees, and transporting timber and other supplies across the sea was costly. Therefore it was prudent to reuse valuable building materials. Structures were transported by land or by sea; in the 1880s, in fact, a special "apparatus for moving buildings" was brought from New Bedford to the island on a schooner."[7]

Although valiant attempts were made to keep whaling alive and to establish businesses, including the manufacturing of shoes, there was a sense of foreboding in the town that the island would become a poor fishing village. The Civil War further interrupted life when Nantucket men answered the call to arms in the summer of 1861. One Nantucketer, writing in 1874, looked back to this dismal time period in the island's history and gave the following description: "[T]he good old town was going sadly to decay, putting on the air of seediness...houses were devoid of paint...a new house was a wonder that the entire population turned out to see and carefully watched every step of its progress; while many dwellings appeared to be on their last legs, and very poor specimens of legs they were;...the price of real estate was so low that a house and land would scarcely bring the cost of newly shingling the roof of the dwelling; many houses could not be rented at all...."[8]

Salvation came in the form of tourism. Remarkably, even as early as 1847 Nantucket was becoming known as a summer resort. The Nantucket *Inquirer and Mirror* reported that year: "It is very evident that people abroad are rapidly making the discovery that Nantucket is about the most pleasant and comfortable place of resort during the summer months that can be found within the limits 'of these United States.' For years the number of pleasure travellers [sic] visiting our island has been steadily increasing, and this year the tide has set in more strongly than ever before. People are coming from every part of the country, to breathe our pure and invigorating air, to enjoy our unequalled scenery, to bathe, walk, ride, have *squantums*—in a word to enjoy themselves, as they can most thoroughly."[9]

In the mid-1860s the editors of the Nantucket *Inquirer and Mirror* newspaper ran editorials encouraging islanders to invest in the summer trade; later articles appeared in national periodicals that spread the word concerning the island's attributes as a summer resort (FIGURE 14). By the early 1870s the new era of tourism began in earnest: new dwellings began to be erected, older homes were updated to appeal to boarders, streets were improved, and ferry service—linked to railroad lines to Boston and New York—increased to two boats a day in the summer, to accommodate the growth in the number of visitors (FIGURE 15). As historian William F. Macy noted, carpenters from off island had to be brought over to keep up with the building boom, and soon "something like prosperity dawned once more."[10]

FIGURE 13: 21 Cliff Road Being Moved, ca. 1900. *House moves on the island became a common occurrence beginning in the early nineteenth century, a result of Yankee thrift and the prohibitive cost of shipping building supplies from the mainland. As developer Edward Underhill noted in 1888, every house on the island seems never to be satisfied unless it has occupied at least two places during its existence.* Courtesy of the Nantucket Historical Association.

FIGURE 14: Nantucket Harbor, from the Church Tower, 1873. *Originally printed in "Nantucket," Scribner's Monthly, vol. VI, no. 4 (August 1873), 389. Illustrated articles touting Nantucket's attributes, published in popular periodicals, contributed to the growth of the island's summer resort industry. In 1873, a writer for* Scribner's *claimed that Nantucket was the most quaint and interesting seaboard town in America "on account of the reminiscences of the past which one constantly meets in every ramble."* Courtesy of Spinner Publications, Inc.

FIGURE 15: Steamboat Wharf, Nantucket, in the Late Nineteenth Century. *By the mid-1870s, two steamboats a day made trips to Nantucket in the summer, bringing hundreds of visitors. The daily arrival of these ships at Steamboat Wharf was an exciting and much anticipated event for both visitors and Nantucket residents. As one 1882 guidebook noted, visitors were met at the wharf by "hackmen, teamsters, and expressmen,—the jolliest, kindest, and wittiest set of human beings upon the face of the globe,—ready to take you and your luggage to any hotel or boarding-house which you may have selected."* Courtesy of the Nantucket Historical Association.

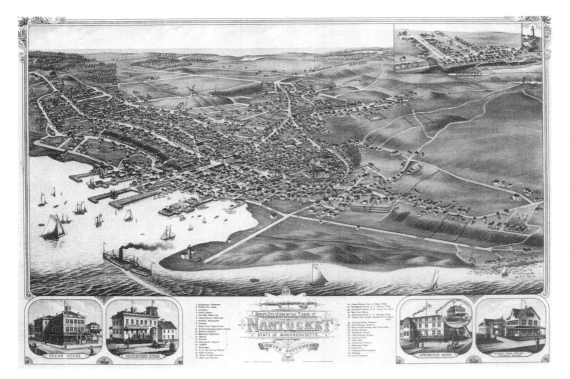

{ LEFT }

FIGURE 16: Bird's Eye
View of the Town of
Nantucket, State of
Massachusetts, Looking
Southwest, 1881. *Litho-
graph, published by J. J.
Stoner, printed by Beck &
Pauli, Madison, Wisconsin.
By 1880 Nantucket was "on
the map" as a summer
resort, inspiring the production of this bird's-eye vista,
sold to tourists for two dollars. The waterfront is
bustling with pleasure sailing craft and a steamship
bringing tourists from the
mainland; railroad tracks
can be seen in the far distance; new homes built for
summer tourists can be seen
on the "Cliff" and large
hotels figure prominently
along the lower edge of the
map.* Courtesy of the Nantucket
Historical Association.

{ OPPOSITE }

FIGURE 17: "Dexioma,"
The Captain George
Wilber House, 'Sconset.
*Built in the first half of the
eighteenth century, this rose-
covered cottage is a lovely
example of a fishing shack
that was later turned into a
vacation home.*

By the 1880s, the new tourism industry gave rise to rampant land speculation and building activity across the island; "off islanders" snapped up oceanfront property on which to build their spacious
summer cottages in the latest mode (FIGURE 16). Following national trends, eclectic Victorian
homes, ranging from Gothic Revival to the creative Shingle style, were erected by island builders.

The small fishing village of Siasconset (generally referred to as 'Sconset), established in the late
seventeenth century at the eastern end of the island (FIGURE 17), became increasingly popular as the
preferred summer resort spot (FIGURE 18), or as one writer suggested, "the brightest gem city of rest
and enjoyment on the New England coast."[11] Until the summer of 1884, 'Sconset was reached from
town by way of carriage, a bumpy forty-five-minute ride across eight miles of commons and moors.
When the island's railroad was extended to the village of 'Sconset in July of 1884, and became the
favored mode of transport, the trains first ran across the fragrant moors to Surfside and then followed
a beautiful path along the seashore. The newspaper reported that the railroad and building boom

FIGURE 18: Ocean View House Hotel, 'Sconset Village, ca. 1890. *The exuberant nature of Victorian architecture seemed to match the mood of pleasure seekers in 'Sconset during the late nineteenth century.* Courtesy of the Nantucket Historical Association.

were welcome sights: "A new era appears to have dawned upon the once quiet, slumbering village and its people, and they welcome the sound of the locomotive, and the arrival of new faces, as evidences of continued prosperity."[12] The predominant styles of architecture of the Victorian period, which reflected this new prosperity, can still be seen along the village's byways and lanes.

By the end of the nineteenth century, Nantucket's image, as well as its appeal to visitors, was closely linked to its historic structures, which had become symbols of the island's romantic past.[13] This was due in part to the fascination of some Americans for "all that was not modern, urban, and industrialized," including historic buildings and preindustrial village life.[14] As Nantucket transformed itself into a "famous watering-place" and provided new amenities for tourists, including the railroad, enormous hotels, and a plethora of seaside cottages, it endangered the island's historic legacy. Some islanders lamented the growth and subsequent loss of the "queer old houses of ancient date" and the charm of the island, which they saw "gradually passing away before the triumphal march of modern improvement and innovation."[15] Efforts were soon made to protect the island's historical artifacts and buildings. In 1894 a group of concerned citizens founded the Nantucket Historical Association, in order to "secure all possible material relating to old Nantucket...before it is too late and those valuable mementos are carried away from the island."[16]

The early twentieth century brought some progress to the island, including expanded electricity and cable, regular airplane service, and, after years of struggle against it, the automobile. Colonial Revival–style architecture, and the modern convenience of practical "mail-order" bungalows appealed to Nantucketers at that time and became popular house types. However, some innovations of the twentieth century, from traffic lights to gaudy neon signs, never took hold on Nantucket.

As the twentieth century progressed, steps were taken toward establishing design restrictions and regulations for all new island structures. In the late 1930s, more than thirty island architects, builders, artisans, realtors, building suppliers, and homeowners joined together to sign an agreement to offer plans and architectural advice to builders of new homes in order to preserve the "Colonial character" of Nantucket.[17] Their efforts began in 1937 with a conference and an analysis of 320 historic homes on the island, which resulted in Everett Crosby's book *95% Perfect*, the object of which was to "keep unmarred the old Nantucket dwellings."[18]

In 1955, the Historic District and Historic District Commission (HDC) were established on the island. Eleven years later the National Park Service, part of the United States Department of the Interior, designated the town a National Historic Landmark, and subsequently Nantucket was listed in the National Register of Historic Places. The HDC's landmark *Building With Nantucket in Mind* was published in 1978, providing architects, builders, and homeowners specific guidelines for building new structures on the island.

Despite all the restrictions established by the HDC, several renowned architects from the mainland were able to build significant examples of innovative postmodern structures in remote locations around the island. Robert Venturi, John Rauch, and Graham Gund are among the award-winning architects who have successfully designed homes on Nantucket that are a hybrid of innovation, historical influences, and stylistic features required by the town's design guidelines.

When walking through town or on a ramble along the winding lanes of 'Sconset, make note of the interesting architectural elements of each building, for each feature, each house has a story to tell. And remember that the preservation of Nantucket's historic architecture is in all of our hands. As one architectural historian so aptly wrote, "The vitality of history is everywhere in Nantucket. It draws distinction to life today, and provides a reminder of times past. Such survival is a fortunate accident of time and history; and its continuance lays grave responsibilities on us and succeeding generations."[19]

{ OPPOSITE }
FIGURE 19:
The Mayflower, Built ca. 1894, Baxter Road, 'Sconset. *At the end of the nineteenth century, the free-form, uniquely American Shingle style appeared on the island, ushering in the modern era of architecture on Nantucket.*

Hearth and Home:
The Lean-to House

Rose Gonnella

*W*INTER, Nantucket Island. A strong wind whistles off the Atlantic from the northwest. The air is damp with salt spray; the sun dips out of sight by four o'clock. Dry warmth is an imperative. Enter the kitchen of an early-eighteenth-century dwelling on Nantucket. A fire is burning in the enormous hearth, an aromatic soup simmers in an iron pot hanging from the trammel over the fire.

The fundamental heating and cooking hearth built for the seventeenth- and early-eighteenth-century "dwelling houses" on Nantucket, and across the Massachusetts Bay Colonies, ranged from seven to nine feet in width, with a height of over four feet. This immense fireplace, large enough to stand in, was the structural anchor of the house (FIGURE 1). Seen from virtually any street in the town of Nantucket, a centrally placed, colossal, square chimneystack at the ridge line of the roof is one unmistakable characteristic of an older home on Nantucket. Fortunately, the island today has approximately forty residences that are gracious survivors of

FIGURE 1: Fireside, 1944, at the Elihu Coleman House, Built in 1722. *During the seventeenth and eighteenth centuries, the hearth functioned as a cooking and heating appliance. Immense as it may be, the fireplace was not an efficient source of heat. The romantic idea of the great hearth being the heart of the home was a nineteenth-century notion, created long after heating systems improved. Still capable of functioning many generations after construction, the hearths found in old houses continue to be preserved and enjoyed for their historic value.* Photograph by B. Anthony Stewart. Courtesy of the National Geographic Magazine Image Collection.

{ OPPOSITE }
FIGURE 2: The Elihu Coleman House, Built in 1722, Hawthorne Lane, ca. 1900. *Withstanding the sea winds for more than two hundred years and still surrounded by precious open space, this outstanding example of a lean-to style house allows the imagination to conjure visions of old Nantucket.* Courtesy of the Nantucket Historical Association.

FIGURE 3: "Wetu." Illustration by Rose Gonnella, 2003. *Wampanoag Indians of Nantucket were likely to have erected dwellings such as the one pictured. Called "wigwams" by the English, this house type was in use by the indigenous population of New England.*

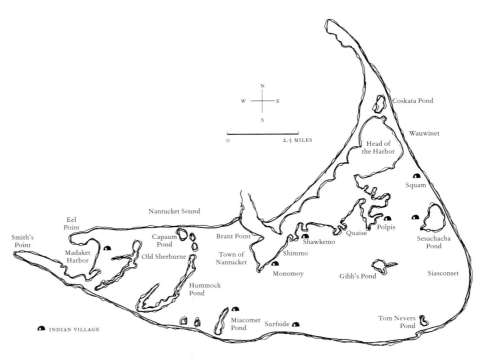

FIGURE 4: Nantucket Island. Illustration by Rose Gonnella and Dilek Katgi, 2003. *This map shows the early English settlement at Sherburne and the locations of the Wampanoag Indian settlements.*

the early-eighteenth-century settlement of the island (FIGURE 2).[1] Derived from postmedieval old-world designs, adapted to the climate and resources of the New World, influenced by particular cultural forces, and preserved by both tradition and chance, the historic architecture of Nantucket is the legacy of a group of staunchly individualistic and spirited people who lived on a notable island twenty-four miles from the mainland shore and three thousand miles from their original home across the Atlantic Ocean.

The first Europeans to colonize Nantucket were entrepreneurial Englishmen from the south and eastern regions of England, who first settled north of Boston. Thomas Macy, Edward Starbuck, and Tristram Coffin were among the leaders of a small group seeking viable farmland and a local governing system of their own design, different from the intrusive Puritan order from which they hailed. Nantucket proved a sound choice. When the colonization of Nantucket began in 1659,[2] the first settlers found that the island was no "howling desart [where] the onely encouragements were the laborious breaking up of bushy ground, with the continued toyl of erecting houses," as New England was described in 1628 by Edward Johnson in his long essay, *Wonder-working Providence.* Nantucket was known to the English inhabitants on Martha's Vineyard who brought livestock to graze there. Among the Vineyarders was the governor and missionary Thomas Mayhew, who owned both islands as part of a royal grant. Mayhew eventually sold Nantucket to the Macy-Coffin group. Importantly, Nantucket was also home to several established groups of Wampanoag Indians. The approximately three thousand native Nantucketers had villages strategically established across the island and were living in arbor-like dwellings made of bent wood and grass mats (what the English called "wigwams") (FIGURE 3). The Wampanoags gathered abundant shellfish, foraged native fruits, and grew corn. They were also proficient fishermen and captured whales that drifted along the beach, skills that were to become especially profitable to the English inhabitants.[3] The settlers chose Nantucket in part because the grass-covered island was particularly suited to the raising of sheep, a livelihood with which they were familiar. But with guidance from the native islanders, the sea eventually provided a most lucrative enterprise for the English.[4]

None of the houses built by the first purchasers, Coffin, Macy, Starbuck, and others, during the earliest decades of Nantucket's colonization exist on site as originally built. Many of Nantucket's seventeenth-century structures are recorded to have been moved[5] from their original location near Capaum Harbor, when storm-driven sands finally closed access to Nantucket Sound in 1717 (FIGURE 4). Houses in this north-westerly region (Sherburne was renamed Nantucket in 1795) were relocated a mile east to a larger harbor around which the present town of Nantucket developed. In an environment where large trees were severely limited and most timber, lumber, and supplies were brought from off island, it was highly prudent to reuse valuable building materials.[6] In a 1714 entry in his carpenter's account book, Richard Macy (1689–1779) noted, "bargined with old Joseph [R]usel for carting my frame and the timber." Macy may be referring to the frame of a house off-loaded from a ship or perhaps from an intra-island move.[7]

During the early years of colonization, carpenter John Bishop, a partner of the island's original purchasers who had been recruited from the mainland specifically for his building skills, erected heavy timber-frame, single- and double-room, postmedieval English-style[8] dwellings for the families of Massachusetts emigrants at Sherburne. These late-seventeenth-century dwellings, with a central chimney and baffle-entry plan, were a continuum of the vernacular architecture that was previously known from the colonists' homeland.[9] Noted English historian R. W. Brunskill explains the visual clues of the style: "The baffle-entry house plan may easily be recognized from the outside. If one draws an imaginary line down from the principle chimney stack and it falls within the width of the front doorway then the plan has been used.... Some houses of this plan have two living units on each floor... there is a kitchen/living room to one side of the entrance lobby and fireplace stack and a heated parlor to the other side. The arrangement is rarely completely symmetrical because the kitchen living room and its chamber [above] are normally wider than the parlour and parlour chamber."[10]

One example illustrating several features of the early English dwelling type remains in the town of Nantucket today at 139 Main Street (FIGURE 5). Built sometime before 1690,[11] the house was

FIGURE 7: Captain Richard Gardner III House, Built ca. 1722–24, 34 West Chester Street. *An asymmetrical gable is the unmistakable architectural feature of the lean-to house. Captain Gardner built this house as an integral lean-to.*

{ OPPOSITE }

FIGURE 5: Richard Gardner II House, Built Before 1690, 139 Main Street. *Clad from top to bottom in shingles, this house illustrates several key characteristics of the English style of the seventeenth century: small, diamond-pane casement windows and massive chimney. The house was in the Gardner family for more than two hundred years.*

{ ABOVE }

FIGURE 6: Building Details. Illustration by Rose Gonnella, pencil on paper, 1995. *A flat board door with long, strap hinges and a wooden string-latch are characteristic features of seventeenth-century homes on Nantucket.*

moved five hundred feet from its construction site and restored in the 1920s.[12] Initial ownership of the home is attributed to either Richard Gardner II (1653–1728) or his son, Joseph (1677–1747), descendants of Richard Gardner I (1626–?), a seaman and partner of the initial purchasers of the island. Originally one room deep with two and a half stories, this house was later extended to the side and rear. Exterior details express its English colonial character.[13] The typically small, hinged casement windows are set with leaded, diamond-pane glass. Doors are of plain boards with long, metal strap hinges and a wooden latch (FIGURE 6). Aligned with the front entrance and crowning the steeply pitched roof is a massive, articulated chimneystack.

As building design progressed to accommodate growing families, the single- or double-room English house was extended at the rear to its northern side, and at times laterally as well, as exhibited at the Richard Gardner II house. The rear extension, with its characteristic single sloping roof, is known as a "lean-to".[14] On Nantucket, the lean-to is the distinct building feature that defines both the shed-like extension and the entire style of the house. As it did on the mainland, the practical and often essential lean-to became integral to the plan and construction of the home (FIGURE 7). Gradually, the one-room-deep, original English house evolved into two-room-deep variations (FIGURE 8). The insular Nantucketers held fast to the structurally simple and sensible lean-to house. The design reached a height of popularity between 1700 and 1760 with small, one-and-three-quarter-story versions persisting into the early 1900s (FIGURE 9).

The sprawling early-eighteenth-century settlement of Sherburne does not exist today, but tiny hints of its rural aspect can still be glimpsed at several Nantucket homes including the Captain Richard Gardner III house, circa 1722–24,[15] at 34 West Chester Street (FIGURE 10); the Major Josiah Coffin house, circa 1724, at 90 North Liberty Street (FIGURE 11); the Charles Gardner house, circa 1740, on Quarter Mile Hill[16] (FIGURE 12); and the Elihu Coleman house, built in 1722 on Hawthorne Lane—the last to be built in the "old" Sherburne site (FIGURE 1). Notably, Coleman was a carpenter who built his own house. He was an outspoken member of the Religious Society of Friends, or Quakers, and published an early abolitionist tract in 1733.[17]

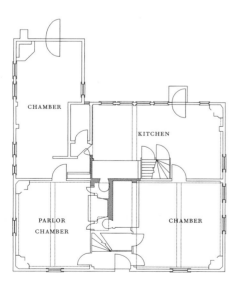

{ LEFT }

FIGURE 8: Floor Plan of the Christopher Starbuck House, Constructed and Extended ca. 1690–1757. Illustration by Richard Valdes, 2003. *When the house was moved to its present location in 1757, the western room (in the lower left of the plan) and rear lean-to section were added. Note that there are recessed bake ovens in the hearths of both the kitchen and front chamber, an indication that suggests the rear kitchen was added at a later date.*

{ ABOVE }

FIGURE 9: One-and-a-Half-Story Lean-to of the Late-Nineteeth Century on Atlantic Avenue. *Adopted from the mainland standard and used on Nantucket long after it lost popularity in New England, the lean-to model persisted on the island for over a half a century.* Courtesy of the Nantucket Historical Association.

{ OPPOSITE }

FIGURE 10: Captain Richard Gardner III House, Built ca. 1722–24 at 34 West Chester Street. *This house is a testimony to the durability of timber-frame construction, as it was built for the Gardner family 280 years ago. Historian Henry Worth aptly notes the appeal of the direct and honest design of these lean-to houses: "[They have] to a high degree that subtle quality, called 'atmosphere,' that attracts and satisfies the eye of all."*

{ OPPOSITE }

FIGURE 11: Major Josiah Coffin House, Built ca. 1724, 90 North Liberty. *Maritime Nantucketers were so adamant about the accuracy of southern orientation that they would set the foundation posts by compass. For instance, in the nineteenth century Professor Henry Mitchell investigated the age of the Josiah Coffin house by means of a compass. He computed a building date of 1723 as the date when the east and west sides of that house coincided with the magnetic north. Mitchell conferred with the woman who owned the property and found he had a successful estimate.*

{ ABOVE }

FIGURE 12: Charles Gardner House, Built ca. 1740, Quarter Mile Hill. *Tucked away on a quiet lane off Main Street and facing south, this mid-eighteenth-century-style home is a transitional type of lean-to. The chimney and front door alignment indicates the lean-to plan, but the rear wall has a two full stories. Within a few decades after the Gardner home was built, the lean-to lost favor and this full, two-and-a-half-story house was popularly adopted. The section on the east end is a twentieth-century addition.* Courtesy of the Nantucket Historical Association.

Each of these solid houses is situated away from the street at seemingly random angles and surrounded by generous open space. Instead of facing the road in an orderly manner, the earliest houses were oriented to the south and therefore many of the facades cannot be easily seen by the passerby (FIGURE 10). Choosing a southern orientation was far from random. Collecting solar warmth, the south-facing facade absorbed strong rays of the sun into the primary rooms of the house, and the long sloping roof on the north side, known as a "catslide," buffeted the wind. Henry C. Forman, a respected historian of early Nantucket architecture, has noted: "[t]he catslide was generally placed on the north side because the prevailing southwest wind tended to tear off fewer shingles than would be the case if the structure faced the other way. What Islander, besides, would wish to see his valuable shingles flying away like birds in the sky?"[18]

Nantucket Town's remarkable cache of eighteenth-century lean-to houses—several of which have passed down through eight or nine generations of the same family—represents a significant archive of American vernacular architecture. As noted in deeds and probate records kept at Nantucket's town hall, the Christopher Starbuck house (FIGURES 8, 13, 14), built circa 1690–1757, at 105 Main Street, was kept in the family for 175 years. The Starbucks were among the most influential families in early Nantucket.[19] Christopher Starbuck (1731–1815) was the great-grandson of Mary Starbuck (1645–1717), the charismatic woman who was instrumental in establishing the Society of Friends on Nantucket.[20] The house, moved from the first seventeenth-century Sherburne site and enlarged, faces south and was originally the early English type with each floor one room deep. It was expanded to the west and north sometime before 1757,[21] resulting in a larger, three-bay (building division) facade with two front windows, one on either side of the entrance (FIGURE 13).

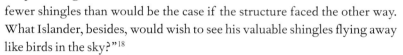

{ OPPOSITE }

FIGURE 13: Christopher Starbuck House, Built ca. 1690–1757, 105 Main Street. *Built facing south before orientation to the street was necessary, this house sits firmly on the ground counterpoint to the road. The gable dormers on the lean-to roof are a twentieth-century addition.*

{ ABOVE }

FIGURE 14: Facade of the Christopher Starbuck House. *Once given a Victorian hooded door detail and other late-nineteenth-century ornaments, the entrance to the Starbuck house was restored in the early twentieth century to the aesthetically appropriate simple board door of the period in which the house was built.*

The humble and dignified Starbuck house, restored and preserved with respect to its history, is a perfect mirror of Nantucket's sturdy lean-to architecture. A sill flush with the ground, a heavy post-and-beam frame built around a giant chimney, exposed timbers on the interior; and a baffle-entry plan are the chief characteristics inherited from the English dwelling phase. The lean-to is a full two rooms deep. Two stories high in front with a catslide roof sloping down to one story in the rear, the Starbuck house displays the asymmetrical gable end that is the hallmark of the lean-to.

Two types of the lean-to can be found on Nantucket. The first is a full-house, built with two rooms in front (parlor and chamber)—one on either side of the central chimney—and three rooms in the rear, including a narrow pantry, kitchen, and secondary chamber. Examples of this style include the Josiah Coffin house (a five-bay version) and the Captain Richard Gardner III house (a three-bay version). The second lean-to type is the smaller, half-size house, containing a single front room (a parlor with two windows) and two rear chambers (kitchen and pantry) (FIGURE 15). The chimney of the half-house is aligned with the front door and abuts a side wall. This smaller variation was meant to eventually be expanded laterally into a full-house such as the Christopher Starbuck house. In the case of the Richard Swain house, however, built circa 1755, at 3 Weymouth Lane,[22] only a small shed was added to the west side because the lot could not accommodate a full-size room.

On the mainland, the lean-to was generally nicknamed a "saltbox" in reference to the shape of containers that held that mineral. The outside form and interior plan of the lean-to closely followed that of New England models. Despite similarities, several architectural features widely found in the two-story English houses and the lean-to houses built in the seventeenth- and early-eighteenth-century Massachusetts colonies were absent from their Nantucket counterparts. For instance, large facade gables, projecting first-floor porches, and second-floor overhangs (or jetties), with their decorative drop pendants, and deep eaves did not appear on Nantucket's seventeenth- and eighteenth-century houses.[23] From the beginning, the defining character of the island's vernacular architecture had been an overriding sense of restraint. The stark minimalism of the Nantucket form stems, in part, from circumstances of isolation. On an island where most building materials needed to be imported, restraint was an economic reality. Though not poor, the entrepreneurial colonists were practical by necessity. As one might anticipate, weather also had its influence. Absent are the roof overhangs that were commonly incorporated into mainland homes.[24] Perhaps there was the fear of a strong Nantucket wind catching hold under the overhang and pulling apart the roof.

Practical restraint used in homebuilding may have gained momentum with the fledgling maritime economy by way of house carpenters who also worked constructing and repairing boats.[25] The efficient use of materials and space employed in boat building found its way into the construction of houses.[26] Furthermore, the functionally spare style fit the virtue of simplicity espoused by the growing popula-

{ OPPOSITE }

FIGURE 15: Richard Swain House, Built ca. 1755, 3 Weymouth Lane. *Unlike a full lean-to with two front rooms, there is only one front room in this half-house. Nonetheless, the living area is comfortable in size and receives generous sunlight through the two south-facing windows.*

tion of the Society of Friends, who were beginning to exert influence over taste and propriety. The Friends' principles guided the faithful to live and dress humbly and to extend this outlook to the design of their homes. The conservative exterior and the low rear wall of the lean-to style tempered the massiveness and perceived ostentation of the form, thus soothing the Quaker mind-set.[27] The islanders, consciously or not, achieved an overall aesthetic harmony through collective acceptance of the notion that less was economically and appropriately more. The Quakers shunned worldly opulence, but they were progressive in terms of technology, such as heating, and probably lighting, within the home.[28]

The virtue of simplicity and ship-tight efficiency did not prevent the natural pursuit of comfort for Nantucketers. The lean-to plan expanded living space by providing new utility rooms on the first floor at the rear, chambers for storage and small living spaces on the second, and even a third-floor garret.[29] The easily recognizable asymmetrical gable of the lean-to, the massive ridge chimney, and the window arrangement on the facade reflect the house plan within. As with its English house predecessor, access to the baffle-entry lean-to is immediate and without formality. The board door opens directly into a narrow vestibule, then called a porch (FIGURE 16). Directly opposite the door, steeply winding stairs wrap around the huge internal chimney. A new feature of the front entrance—a five-pane transom across the top of the door—illuminates the tiny interior porch.[30] Transom lights might also be found above each of the doors leading to the interior rooms as an aid in the detection of harmful fires.[31] Perfectly suited for windswept regions, the minimal enclosed entry blocked damp sea breezes from sweeping through the house.[32]

On either side of the vestibule, the plan included a single room—a chamber for sleeping and a parlor for receiving guests, each with a fireplace. The rear utility rooms were reached through the front parlor and comprised a small chamber, a buttery or milkroom (a pantry), and the kitchen, with its giant hearth and built-in bake oven (FIGURES 17, 18). A circular cellar below the kitchen kept food cool all year round.

On the exterior, architectural details contributed to the distinguishing fabric of the whole structure. As noted previously, seventeenth- and early-eighteenth-century houses were originally constructed with small, diamond-paned casement windows and flat board doors with wooden latches and long, wrought-iron, strap hinges. Latches, hinges, and board doors continued to be used into the eighteenth century and can be seen on many lean-to houses. As on the mainland, window construction styles improved as technology and finances advanced. Fixed or swinging casements with leaded panes were replaced with larger double-hung sashes entirely of wood. On the lean-to houses throughout Nantucket Town, the small twelve-over-twelve-pane sash windows are another clue in recognizing the earliest structures, as seen at the Alex and George Folger house, built before 1750, at 10 Ash Street[33] (FIGURE 19).

FIGURE 16: Interior "Porch," Major Josiah Coffin House, Built ca. 1724, 90 North Liberty. *The tiny vestibule of this house contains steep winding stairs behind vertical board sheathing. This baffle-entry keeps the Nantucket wind from blowing through the house. On an island that is statistically one of the windiest spots on the East Coast, blocking the wind was a priority.*

{ TOP }

FIGURE 17: Eastman Johnson, Susan Ray's Kitchen—
Nantucket, 1875. Oil on board. *A nineteenth-century painter*
of the American scene who summered on Nantucket, Johnson
depicted Susan Ray (1821–1904) emerging from the tiny milk
room in the lean-to addition of her home at 9 Mill Street. The
simplicity of the room was a symbol of humility, an important
ethic of the Religious Society of Friends (Quakers). Courtesy
of the Addison Gallery of American Art, Phillips Academy, Andover,
Massachusetts. Gift of John K. McMurray in memory of Dr. James
Graham Leyburn, 1994.69.

{ BOTTOM }

FIGURE 18: Eastman Johnson, The Other Side of Susan
Ray's Kitchen—Nantucket, ca. 1875. Oil on paper board.
The spare character of the room emerges in Johnson's skilled
and precise brushwork: he portrays the plaster walls, wooden
doors, paneling, heavy beams, and hearth of Susan Ray's
kitchen. Courtesy of the Addison Gallery of American Art, Phillips
Academy, Andover, Massachusetts. Museum Purchase, 1996.74.

Many of the various construction materials and techniques of eighteenth-century Nantucket houses are noted in the account books of the island carpenters. Among the many building notations recorded in the accounts of island builder Richard Macy is an entry dated 1718 for "making 3 windo frames and 3 casements."[34] Later in the century, carpenters' account books frequently record the making of sashes but there are no references to casement windows. For instance, in his ledger begun in 1788, Benjamin Newland records: "10 window frames" and "210 Squares of Sashes" for Elisha Barnet, and "putting 75 Squairs of Sash" for Samuel Howland.[35] Recorded by John Coffin in 1790: ten days labor on Simeon Ellis's house including, "8 window frame, 24 squars sashis, 4 squars sashes for over door." The latter entry notes the specific use of transom lights.[36]

Although leaded-pane casements were not employed in the lean-to houses built shortly after 1700, the pegged heavy plank-frame and pegged construction of the window was retained. This pegged-together form was easily fitted or tapped out if the building was expanded or moved.[37]

Exterior cladding, perhaps more than any other single component, establishes the character of Nantucket's architecture. Strikingly noticeable and widespread even today, split shingles over horizontal sheathing was preferred as the primary cladding rather than the clapboards that were favored on the mainland. Tightly spaced clapboards, once termed "clinker-built" on Nantucket,[38] did have a place. However, pine or cedar shingles, which do not need to be painted, offer superior durability in the maritime climate by clamping out the wind and stubbornly resisting saltwater spray.[39] Toiling over the wind and wear on a house is clearly recorded by carpenter John Coffin in his account book entry of 1790. His work on Laban Gardner's house included: "laber to stop out wind from garret to celler[,] mend position [of] celler and milkroom shelves…take up harth in c [chamber] room & lay it again[,] lay floar in w [west] room and mend under floar and mend kitchen floar."[40]

Shingles are mentioned with great frequency in carpenter account books. In 1718, Richard Macy noted the cost of four thousand "shingls."[41] In 1789, Benjamin Newland noted one and three-quarter "thousand of shingels" for Ebenezer Baley. Newland also charged Goodspeed Jones for two thousand shingles "dlivard,"[42] while carpenter John Coffin asked twelve shillings of Simeon Ellis for "laber shingle fore side house."[43]

A pure "saltbox" house is a rarity on the island, as most have what are called "warts"—single-slope roof additions or outshuts projecting from the side of the house and the rear beyond the lean-to. In addition, many of the eighteenth-century houses had their one-story rear walls later raised in height, obliterating the lean-to. Altered, extended, or outwardly pushed in some way, the lean-to houses all have additions built to accommodate modern kitchens and new bedrooms, sunrooms, or dens (FIGURE 20). Fortunately these warts, ells, or dormers are generally discreet and well integrated

{ OPPOSITE }

FIGURE 19: Alex and George Folger House, Built Before 1750, 10 Ash Street. *Covered with vine roses, this striking five-bay facade does not face the street; instead it faces south to collect the warmth of the sun. The plank windows—slightly projecting from the face of the building—and board door with long strap hinges are unmistakable details of the early lean-to houses. The present owner of the house, Dr. Bryon Lingeman, suggests that during the early nineteenth century the house was converted into a duplex by two brothers, Alex and George Folger. Partitioning walls have been removed, exposing a long double fireplace.*

{ OPPOSITE }
FIGURE 20: Thomas Macy House, Built ca. 1717, 3 Tattle Court. *Originally a half-house, the Macy house is a south-facing lean-to found on a tiny lane off Fair Street. The original section is recognizable, though the east gable of the house projects a rather large extension that obscures the original salt-box shape. The tall, articulated chimney and slightly project-ing, plank-frame windows are features of its early date.*

{ ABOVE }
FIGURE 21: Interior, Christopher Starbuck House, Built ca. 1690. *Except for several houses owned by the Nantucket Historical Association, Nantucket's historic architecture is in private hands and not accessible by the public. Occasionally, however, a house will be open for a public tour as part of a fund-raising event. In 1945, the Starbuck house was listed on a public tour, and a description of the interior appeared in the island's newspaper: "The exposed floor joists, the oaken sum-mers, girts and corner posts, the huge fireplaces and mantles, the pine floors, provide a splendid, living picture of how those early Nantucket families lived their simplified existence." The house was opened to the public again in 2003.*

at the back of the house (FIGURE 13). The rear jumble and pile of extensions often contribute to the charm and layered history of the houses.

Despite its austere exterior appearance, the lean-to's interior is inviting. Upon walking into the front chamber of the Swain house, the Starbuck house, or the Captain Gardner house, for instance, there is a sense of comfortable inti-macy. Low ceilings, which minimize efforts to heat the space, are practical and snug, yet the rooms are spacious. The interior also reveals building techniques and taste. Decoration is minimal, wood trim around interior doors and windows is nonexistent. The timber-frame con-struction is visible in the exposed beams, posts, and floor joists. Many kitchen timbers were left rough, leaving the slashes of a broad ax and various hand tools visible on the wood's surface. To offer a refined appearance, the exposed beams were planed and have a beaded edge, and corner posts were molded into curved, bracketed shapes before fitting into the framework. These details are seen both in the Starbuck and Swain houses (FIGURES 21, 22, 23). Although the lack of wood trim, the exposed joists, posts, and rough-hewn timbers may appear crude to some contemporary sensibilities, the visible marks of the hand tools reveal some-thing of the fascinating story of the builders, as well as the taste and practi-cal concerns of the people who occupied the homes. By mid-century, many house interiors had walls and ceilings covered with plaster.[44] Formerly exposed wood was hidden from view because homeowners did not find it fashionable at the time. When the Starbuck house was restored and opened to the public in the 1930s, the following description of the front and rear chambers appeared in the Nantucket *Inquirer and Mirror*: "the huge fire-places in the Breckinridge home astonished many visitors, many expres-sions of delight could be heard at the sight of the wide pine-board mantles, the exposed summers, [beams] girts, and floor beams [joists], which brought out the old time appearance of the well-preserved structure."[45]

{ LEFT }
FIGURE 22:
Interior, Richard Swain
House, Built ca. 1755,
3 Weymouth Lane.
*Although small, this
half-house was thoughtfully
built with subtle decorative
touches, such as beaded
beams and curved post
brackets in the former
kitchen.*

{ OPPOSITE }
FIGURE 23: Interior,
Richard Swain House.
*In place of a mantel there is
molded plaster over the parlor fireplace, finished at the
ceiling edge with a curved
and beaded beam.*

Interior refinements, such as plaster walls, continued later in the eighteenth century, as cabinetmakers created frame-and-panel doors and raised-panel wall sheathing. In addition, lathes were used to fabricate elements of chairs, spinning wheels, and stairwell balusters. The cabinetmakers' work added further polish. The Captain Richard Gardner house, at 34 West Chester Street, has many fine examples of the work of joiners, turners, and cabinetmakers. Most attractive is the raised-panel work and cabinetry surrounding the various fireplaces (FIGURE 24). Also at the Gardner house, a set of vertically twisting stairs was replaced with steps in several, straight flights. The staircase has a molded handrail, turned newel posts, and balusters (FIGURE 25). These details may have been added at a date late in the eighteenth century; nonetheless, the thoughtfully crafted features reflect the engaging evolution of the architecture.

Practical, comfortable, and aesthetically pleasing to the eye of the Nantucketer, the lean-to, both large and small, was a long-favored design. When in the 1730s homes in New England developed into a full two stories at both front and rear, the design was adopted on Nantucket. The idiosyncratic islanders, however, had their own plan for the next phase of home building.

{ OPPOSITE }

FIGURE 24: Interior, Captain Richard Gardner House, Built ca. 1722–24, 34 West Chester Street. *Fine craftsmanship can be found in all aspects of this house, including the entry staircase. Visible here are the extensive raised-panel walls of the living space.*

{ ABOVE }

FIGURE 25: Interior, Captain Richard Gardner House. *The several sets of straight flights of steps, the turned newel post, and balusters in the front vestibule were likely to have been added at a date later than the initial construction of the house. The paneled wood and turned posts are simple refinements; with prosperity came the inclination to make details of the home more elaborate and pleasing to the eye.*

Assembling a Timber Frame

ERIC GRADOIA

FIGURE B: Timber Frame Detail at the Captain Richard Gardner House, Built ca. 1722–24, 34 West Chester Street.
Exposed timbers at the peak of the house reveal the trunnel (peg) that fastens together the mortise-and-tenon joint of a pair of roof timbers.
The board planking used to sheath the building interior was usually whitewashed, and interior walls were given an additional
layer of plaster for insulation and finish. On the exterior, the boarding was covered with an added layer of shingles.

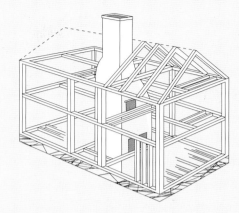

FIGURE A: The Timber Frame. Illustration by Rose Gonnella and Cesar Rubin, 2003. *In New England, a dwelling house was built around a central chimney. Joined together while flat on the ground, wall sections were raised into place to form the structural frame of the building.*

ALTHOUGH BOTH MASONRY WALL CONSTRUCTION of stone and brick and timber-framed, wattle- and daub-filled (lathe and plaster) wall construction were known from the colonists' British homeland, the practice of building in timber was the obvious and natural choice throughout New England, where wide-girth trees were found in great abundance. Despite a lack of significant forests on Nantucket, imported wood timber frame was still the most common building method used for dwellings and commercial structures from the seventeenth through the nineteenth centuries.

In simplest terms, timber frame construction is a method of erecting a building with a structural system fabricated from squared timbers connected to one another with joinery. Trees such as the white oak and red pine provide the lengths of timber necessary for building construction, as well as the properties desirable in the wood itself. Wood is an excellent building material for a number of reasons. To start, it is easily worked. It is possible for a standing tree to be felled and hewn into a squared timber by one person using only simple hand tools. More important, the physical properties of wood allow it to function well under the common loads that act on a building—tension, compression, and combinations of these forces. Last, wood is durable as long as it is protected from moisture.

Hewn and squared timbers are first cut into a number of individually sized building members: sills, posts, beams, girts, and plates (FIGURE A). Connecting the members requires complex joints fabricated from the timbers themselves. The specific joinery used for a connection depends on what forces are acting on that location of the frame. Perhaps the most common joint is the mortise and tenon,

where a projecting "tongue" on one timber is fitted to an opening of like dimensions on another timber and fastened with a wooden peg called a trunnel (FIGURE B). A mortise-and-tenon joint performs well in compression but poorly in tension. In locations where a timber is performing a number of tasks or carrying great loads, such as a summer beam, the joinery becomes more intricate. A tusk-tenon joint was commonly used at the ends of a summer beam to join it to the frame. The design of this joint allowed it to both bind the frame together while supporting the weight of heavy loads. The most complicated joinery in the average timber-frame building is often found at the heads of corner posts. It is at this location that the post, plate, tie beam, and roof framing meet and fasten together. To achieve this task a complex connection called the "English tying joint" is used. This compound joint binds the timbers together and resists the mix of forces that act on this location.

After the joints have been fabricated, assembly begins with a series of bents. A bent is a group of vertical (posts) and horizontal (beams) members that form one cross section of the frame. Two bents connected together create a bay, and one or more bays connected together form a box frame, the four walls of the building. Using mortise-and-tenon joints, a roofing system is constructed atop the box frame, completing the structure of the building.

A Religious Ethic Shapes a Community:
Typical Nantucket Houses

Rose Gonnella

{ OPPOSITE }

FIGURE 1: Thomas Starbuck House, Built ca. 1726–90, 11 Milk Street. *The plan of Starbuck's comfortable but modest four-bay house was developed and advanced by members of Nantucket's Society of Friends (or Quakers). Thomas Starbuck was descended from Mary Starbuck, who (as was mentioned in Chapter 1) was instrumental in establishing and advancing Quakerism on the island. When Thomas and his wife, Dinah, had their home on Milk Street, the Friends were a significant force on the island, both politically and socially. Their religious ethic directed them to a life of humble simplicity and practical living.*

*F*OR the curious or casual stroller of Nantucket's historic streets and lanes, the abundance of vernacular architecture built by the island's eighteenth-century English settlers reveals a distinct aesthetic sensibility. Houses of a particular, pleasing simplicity and a rigorous consistency of style create an organized, serene appearance that has come to signify the island. Behind the wonderfully ordered array of these exteriors are the comfortable and supremely functional less-known interiors of these homes. Unseen are the pattern of the rooms, the giant hearths and tidy cabinetry, the wide hand-planed floorboards, the carved wooden pegs joining massive beams and posts, and plaster work that exposes marks of a trowel. Exteriors reflect the taste, style, and order of the period, but the interiors speak of the Nantucketers who built and lived their lives in these homes (FIGURE 1).[1]

In his 1945 book, *Three Bricks and Three Brothers*, island resident and author William E. Gardner describes a tiny yet important historic moment inside a Nantucket home:

Wednesday.
　February 27th 1774.
　Fourth Day.
　The birthday of Joseph Starbuck.
　A mite of humanity on this day, but some day he would be the richest whale merchant on Nantucket and a builder of many ships and three brick mansions for his three sons.
　Dinah, his mother, felt the first birth-pains late in the afternoon. She left the kitchen by the little door at the side of the huge fireplace. She entered a passageway by the warm chimney. In the middle of the passage she stopped and pulled from the "blanket-closet," built into the chimney, a soft warm blanket new from the loom. She snuggled it close to her neck and ear and entered the small bedroom in which all her children had been born.[2]

{ LEFT }
FIGURE 2: Interior,
Thomas Starbuck House.
*The large hearth located in
this former kitchen is an
indication of construction
conventions from the early
1700s. The overall four-bay
plan of the house, however,
reflects the building design
that was popular later in the
century.*[3] Photograph by Jeffrey
Allen, 2002.

{ OPPOSITE }
FIGURE 3: Interior
Passageway, Thomas
Starbuck House. *The nar-
row walkway between front
and rear rooms included a
space behind the kitchen
hearth for both a storage
closet and gun cabinet. With
a location next to the heating source, stored items were
kept dry.* Photograph by Jeffrey
Allen, 2002.

Dinah Starbuck's closets, passageways, fireplace, and little doors exist today nearly as they did that winter afternoon in 1774 (FIGURES 2, 3). The interior of the well-maintained Thomas Starbuck dwelling, built after 1726 and moved in 1790 to 11 Milk Street, has much to say about the life of the former residents. Traditional floor plans, the exposed post-and-beam frame, and interior doorways display the connections of living: rooms for sitting, cooking, and sleeping. Architectural details such as stairways, cabinetry, and closets inform us of the domestic activity. Worn wooden steps vividly expose the pattern of use in the home.

From the mid-1700s to the mid-1800s, Nantucket was a scene of growth and prosperity due to the ever increasing "greasy luck" of the whaling enterprise.[4] It was, in essence, the vigorous industry

and single-mindedness of the island's flourishing Religious Society of Friends (Quakers)[5] that propelled Nantucket into a hugely successful global whaling port. The success of the whale fishery brought an expanding population, and an urban conglomeration developed with streets and lanes tightly lined with houses (FIGURE 4) and industrial buildings. The protective and insular nature of the faraway island and the earnest doctrine of the Society of Friends resulted in an entire community of architecture that has a distinct visual character. During a visit to Nantucket in 1772, writer and historian J. Hector St. John de Crèvecoeur wrote: "Sherborn [sic] is the only town on the island, which consists of about 530 houses... they are all of a similar construction and appearance; plain, and entirely devoid of exterior or interior ornament."[6]

More than just the plain, visual form of its houses, which were essentially early English in derivation and evolution, the Friends' pervading ethic set Nantucket apart from other towns in New England. Although austerity was as much a mainland Puritan principle as it was for the Friends, it may be the Quaker doctrine of spiritual egalitarianism and communality that resulted in the extraordinary number of similarly styled houses that form the heart of the present historic district.

An understanding of the collective, visual direction of the typical Nantucket house begins with the history of the Society of Friends and an examination of their beliefs. On Nantucket, the Friends were in the right place at the right time. They gained a firm foothold and momentum on the island because their individualist, egalitarian practices fit with the independently minded early colonists. During its first fifty years of English inhabitation, Nantucket was home to a group of people tolerant of various religions and of mixed denominations themselves, including Puritans (Congregationalists), Baptists, and "Nothingarians." Some islanders, like Tristram Coffin (a leader of the first purchasers), did not follow any particular religion.[7] Contrary to the unyielding and often punishing Puritan order on the mainland, the early colonists of Nantucket had no tithe laws or conscription to attend any particular church.[8] Notably, no church existed on the island until the Friends built a meeting house in 1711.[9] Distanced by the sea from the mainland Puritans, who persecuted those not following their doctrine, the island was a haven and an ideal ground for an alternative religious order to take root. In the tolerant and isolated atmosphere of Nantucket, the membership of Friends quickly grew.

In a vivid dissertation on the history of the Friends in his book *Quaker Nantucket*, historian Robert Leach illuminates the ethics and doctrines of the religion. He writes that the Friends had an independent character and "denied the authority not only of the clergy but also the primacy of scripture as the sole expression of God's will. Instead, Quakers read the Bible as a manifestation of the Spirit of Truth. They believed that any individual could access the spirit without resort to liturgy, ceremony, doctrine and sacrament."[10]

{ OPPOSITE }

FIGURE 4: Peleg Bunker House, Built ca. 1750, 4 Trader's Lane. *An early version of the typical Nantucket design, this house is surrounded by a ship-rail (capped-picket) fence. Popular on dwellings throughout the town, fences help create a respectful separation between the public way and the private home.*

{ LEFT }

FIGURE 14: Windmill, Built in 1746 by Nathan Wilbur, South Mill Street. *The Mill Street neighborhood was once the location of Nantucket's five windmills which stood on this hilly area at the edge of the town. One of these windmills remains standing and in service for demonstration purposes. It is owned by Nantucket Historical Association and is open as a museum.*

{ RIGHT }

FIGURE 15: Interior Front Hall, 11 Mill Street. *Note the ivory disk at the top of the newel post. It was the custom to celebrate the final payment of the mortgage by installing an ivory disk or "mortgage button" in this prominent location.*

{ LEFT }

FIGURE 16: Hezekiah Swain House, Also Known as the Maria Mitchell House, Built in 1790, 1 Vestal Street. *This typical Nantucket house was built by Hezekiah Swain and owned later (1818) by William Mitchell. It is the birthplace and home of William's daughter, the distinguished astronomer Maria Mitchell. The house is owned by the Maria Mitchell Association and is open to the public as a museum.* Photograph by Margaret Moore Booker, 2002.

{ RIGHT }

FIGURE 17: Maria Mitchell's Study, Built ca. 1830s, 1 Vestal Street. *The small rooms of the typical Nantucket house at times served as much more than a storage area.* Photograph by Patricia Butler, 2002.

second-floor landing (FIGURE 15). With an entrance hall reaching from the front to nearly the rear of the house, each of the rooms are separated for privacy and function.

A feature of the plan particular to Nantucket is the three- to five-foot area between the stairwell and the outside wall of the structure (FIGURE 8). This utilitarian space is divided into a front storage area and a milk-room (pantry), each having a window. The pantry opens onto the kitchen, while the storage space is accessible from the hall. The second-floor plan is identical. The Friends designed an orderly separation of rooms and a comfortable entrance that was practical and useful, unlike some of the grander entrance halls seen in coinciding house styles. In one typical Nantucket house at 1 Vestal Street (FIGURE 16), Quaker William Mitchell (1791–1869) put a small room to very good use. He arranged a study area in the storage space on the second floor (FIGURE 17) for his daughter, Maria Mitchell (1818–1889), who later became a renowned astronomer.

Even within a group of like-minded people, some variations, refinements, and modifications of the typical Nantucket house, such as rear extensions (as seen on 33 Milk Street, FIGURE 7) or the gambrel-roof

FIGURE 18 : View from the Orange Street Bluff of a Gambrel Roof House. *Built during the late 1700s, less than ten of these barn-like houses exist on Nantucket (the one pictured is on Union Street). The design allowed for more space in the second-story rooms but the large roof was not a popular feature on island.* Courtesy of the Nantucket Historical Association.

house (FIGURE 18), were bound to occur.[35] A subtle modification to the form, the Maria Mitchell birthplace, for example, is a mirror image of the Job Macy house. It has the standard seven front windows, but the narrow pantry area is located to the left of the entrance instead of to the right. Window arrangements and interior plans vary slightly, though it is unclear whether these are concurrent or later alterations to the standard. For instance, a typical Nantucket house at 45 India Street (FIGURES 19, 20), constructed circa 1804[36] by carpenter Rescom Taber, is a near twin of the Macy house at 11 Mill Street. Differences exist but are subtle. On the Taber house, the narrow window to the left of the entrance is located on the side of the house rather than the front. In addition, the foundation of the Macy house is flush with the ground; the sill of the Taber house is slightly raised and its front door reached from a small double-sided staircase.

Inside the Taber house, the usual front-hall storage room was not included. Instead, the entrance was left open. Notably, the character of these late-eighteenth-century interiors of the Macy and Taber houses are essentially alike, each having the same basic spatial arrangement and the refinement of plastered and painted walls and raised-panel woodwork (FIGURES 21, 22). The current salmon red, green, blue, and white colors of the walls and doors in these houses would have been appropriate in the early nineteenth century as well (FIGURES 23, 24). A sheaf of Sylvanus Ewer's (1767–1836) financial papers from his life on Nantucket reveals his taste in paint color and may be indicative of the period. Over the course of several years, between 1819 and 1824, Ewer ordered "painting at [his] house" done by Seth Paddock. Ewer does not state whether he was painting the interior or exterior, but his list of colors includes rose pink, blue, green, yellow, black, and "whiting."[37] Although Nantucket has long been known as the "Gray Lady," because of the preponderance of weathered-gray unpainted shingles on the exterior of houses, color was actually common on late-eighteenth-century houses. Phebe Folger (later Mrs. Samuel Coleman, 1771–1857), an educated Nantucket woman, painted two watercolors, circa 1797, of the Pleasant Street area of town (FIGURE 25 and Introduction, FIGURE 2). These watercolors are significant because they show the houses painted red. In a memoir of her childhood, Elizabeth

{ OPPOSITE }

FIGURE 19: Rescom Taber House, Built ca. 1804, 45 India Street. *This subtly modified typical Nantucket house does not have a front window to the right of the door that was common in the design. During the late nineteenth century, the house was given a Victorian "makeover" that included an ornamental door surround with side-windows, a porch, and a bracketed overhang (see Chapter 4, figure 9). Most of the decorative features have been removed. However, the deep overhang and the front door windows remain.*

{ ABOVE }

FIGURE 20: Historic Kitchen, 45 India Street. *Currently filled with antique utensils, this former utilitarian room was an efficient work space when used as a kitchen. The homeowners now use it as a dining room but have occasionally cooked dinners and baked bread in the hearth.*

FIGURES 21 & 22: Front Bedrooms, 45 India Street and 11 Mill Street. *Remarkably similar, these two early-nineteenth-century rooms have raised-panel wall sheathing that is typical of the period. The woodworking creates a simple but attractive finish for the room. The mantel at 45 India Street is a twentieth-century addition.*

FIGURE 23: Parlor, 45 India Street. *Transom lights over the interior doors were a common feature in Nantucket houses, adding much needed light to small spaces. In this case the windows provide illumination to the narrow hall connecting the parlor and rear chamber.*

FIGURE 24: Historic Kitchen, 11 Mill Street. *A finished and plastered ceiling and planed beams were also found in less formal rooms, such as a kitchen. The shelves over the mantle were likely at one time to be a strictly utilitarian feature.*

A Perspective View of part of the town of Nantucket taken from a north window in the house of

FIGURE 25: Phebe Folger, A Perspective View of Part of the Town of Nantucket Taken from a North Window in the House of Walter Folger, ca. 1797. Watercolor on paper. *Folger's illustration of the Pleasant Street neighborhood was drawn from a window in the home of her brother, Walter Folger Jr. Note the three-bay lean-to and the center chimney houses of three and five bays in this watercolor drawing of the town. These residencies indicate the variety of design on the island found along with the typical Nantucket houses.* Courtesy of the Houghton Library, Harvard University.

{ LEFT }

FIGURE 26: Attributed to William Swain, Captain Seth Pinkham (1786–1844), ca. 1844. Oil on panel. *Seth Pinkham came out of retirement to make his last whaling voyage in 1844. It was his final trip, as he died of illness while in the South Pacific.* Courtesy of Nantucket Historical Association. 89.128.1.

{ RIGHT }

FIGURE 27: Captain Seth Pinkham House, Built 1827–28, 40 Fair Street. *A Pinkham descendant, Florence Anderson, writes in her memoir of the ancestral house: "It was . . . a square comely model prevalent in Nantucket through a noteworthy epoch of building. It had two storeys and a half for the main portion, with an ell of two storeys at the back. There was a neatly balustraded "walk" on top and the front steps were arranged in that Flemish manner which the island preferred, with a flight from opposite directions[.]"*

Crosby Bennett (1843–1919) offers an explanation of the exterior house color of the early eighteenth century: "White and green blinds [shutters] was the favorite color scheme. But also many houses were painted red. Few moderns will believe this. Perhaps the fashion came from aping the hue of bricks, a costly building material with us, for every brick had to be transported to our Island by water as a private shipment. You can count on the fingers of two hands our brick buildings."[38]

With the whaling industry booming at the turn of the nineteenth century, homeowners could well afford to expand their houses. Additions at the rear and side were common and can be seen in all of the houses mentioned in this chapter. Many whaling captains built their homes on Orange, India, and Fair streets. Among them was Captain Seth Pinkham (1786–1844, FIGURE 26), who commanded the ships *Dauphin* and *Galen*, and had a home built on Fair Street. The Pinkham house (FIGURE 27) was constructed in 1827–28, in the latter phase of popularity of the typical Nantucket design, and had as part of the original plan a rear kitchen ell with its own fireplace that allowed space for a formal dining area in the middle of the house. With the wealth and worldliness that arrived through whaling to distant lands, came the temptation to live in ways other than what the Friends had originally prescribed. Austerity of form and the limitation of the single, central chimney plan of the four-bay house preferred by the Friends lost favor with those financially capable and aware of more spacious and comfortable room arrangements. Contemporary with the typical Nantucket house, the Federal style was known and welcomed by affluent whaling merchants and successful captains. Islanders chose these larger houses and formal living schemes instead of the traditionally humble Nantucket home. Many dwellings, including the typical Nantucket house, displayed decorative features of the Federal style imposed on windows and especially doors (FIGURE 28).

Indicative of the societal evolution occurring among the affluent, Thomas Starbuck's prosperous son Joseph (1774–1861), a descendant of the island's founding Quaker, Mary Starbuck, was born in a typical Nantucket house. But after being disowned by the Quakers for marrying a nonmember, Joseph built a five-bay, twin-chimney home in 1809 for himself and his family on the appropriately named New Dollar Lane (CHAPTER 3, FIGURE 3). We see in the Joseph Starbuck house a decorative treatment of the front entrance and a more spacious interior plan. Another example is 27 India Street, a typical Nantucket house built circa 1794 for mariner Robert Folger (FIGURE 29). The house has architectural features and decorative elements not common to the style,[39] including a raised basement, a graceful set of double-sided stairs, a panel door with a simple entablature, and unusual wooden quoins[40] on the corners of the structure, all of which combine to project a refined, stately image.

Inevitably, such features that exhibited the status and wealth of their owners replaced the humility and communal equality of the typical Nantucket house. However, the modest-sized, four-bay house without ornament, overhang, or ostentation left an indelible mark on the island. Its aesthetic is responsible for the pleasing proportion and serene simplicity of much of Nantucket's historic architecture.

{ ABOVE }

FIGURE 28: Facade Detail, 40 Fair Street. *Built by prosperous whaling captain Seth Pinkham during the late design phase of the typical Nantucket house, the front entrance of 40 Fair Street displays the refined features common to early-nineteenth-century fashions, including a shelf molding and four-pane transom over the door with graceful attenuated pilasters at each side.*

{ OPPOSITE }

FIGURE 29: Robert Folger House, Built 1794, 27 India Street. *Wooden quoins decorating the edges of this residence echo a masonry feature found in Georgian-style houses on the mainland.*

Ship Shape:
The Influence of Shipbuilding Techniques on Nantucket Architecture

NILES PARKER

Stairwell with Rope Handrail.

NANTUCKET ISLAND'S EXTENSIVE MARITIME history began from a humble start in fishing and shore whaling and developed into an extraordinary global whaling enterprise. Inevitably, Nantucket's unique relationship with the sea found its way into the island's architecture, and it remains evident today in many examples of both exterior and interior design details.

For generations, shipbuilders and carpenters have lived and worked on Nantucket. In fact, the Brant Point shipyard, located near the mouth of Nantucket Harbor, was active at the turn of the nineteenth century, with several ships built there for use in the whaling industry. Recorded in the histories of Nantucket and business account books, many of the island's eighteenth- and nineteenth-century carpenters and joiners who worked on building ships were also constructing houses. Island historian Obed Macy wrote of his grandfather, carpenter Richard Macy, building Nantucket's original Straight Wharf. Richard Macy's own account book of 1718 has several entries that record his work on boats. It is clear that shipbuilding techniques were common knowledge on the island and available to be appropriated into both the construction techniques and the decorative details of house design.

For example, structural devices such as ship's knees, which were braces for the framing of the vessels, are located in many island homes and are borrowed directly from shipbuilding models. A wonderful example exists in the Jethro Coffin house, popularly known as the "Oldest House," built on Sunset Hill in 1686 as a wedding present for Mary Gardner and Jethro Coffin, two descendents of Nantucket's first English families.

In the small and primitive fishing shanties of seventeenth- and eighteenth-century Siasconset, a village on Nantucket's eastern shore, the use of a sleeping loft was an efficient design solution for fully utilizing a tiny space, much like the "below-decks" of a ship. In addition, many of these early fishing shanties, as well as some of the typical Nantucket houses, have narrow vertical stairways and rope handrails that lead to roof walks, fenced platforms located on

Illustration by Henry C. Forman, 1966.

rooftops. While the original purpose of the narrow stairway was to provide easy access to the roof in the event of a chimney fire, their design often echoed the ladders and ropework aboard ships that helped sailors ascend in tight spaces or clamber up masts for a better view. Over the decades many of these small homes have been enlarged, their steep stairways replaced or left unused; but the homes often retain the fanciful nautical details much appreciated today, including porthole windows, ropework, and ivory-decorated railings.

Many of the houses built on Nantucket during its reign as a whaling empire remain as a testimony to practical and sound framing and joining techniques that were also used in shipbuilding. Varying from very real structural design solutions to purely fanciful, decorative touches, evidence of those techniques abound. Perhaps the best example of the latter are the omnipresent quarterboards found on Nantucket homes today. Derivative of the quarterboards that once adorned ships and stated the name of the vessel, these signs are carved with a name for the house or the owner and hung above a door or garage. While perhaps overly quaint, they remain as reminders of the influence that the sea and maritime activity have always had on the architecture and culture of Nantucket.

Whaling Prosperity, Cultural Changes, and Classical Design: Federal and Greek Revival Architecture

Patricia Egan Butler

{ OPPOSITE }

FIGURE 1: Rotch
Counting House,
Built in 1772 at the Foot
of Main Street, Also
Called Market Square.

*A*FTER the Revolutionary War, the United States decidedly sought independence not only from British rule, but also from British custom and culture. This historical period is often described as the beginning of the modern age in this country. Greatly accelerated shipping activity on the nation's coasts and inland waterways resulted in cultural and commercial transportation growth that transformed and established prosperous harbor settlements and river towns. Nantucket and its whaling industry were well positioned to profit from the burgeoning national and international trade opportunities. At the top and bottom of commercial Main Street, the 1772 Rotch Counting House (FIGURE 1) and the 1818 Pacific Bank represent the dramatic economic change on Nantucket that began after the American Revolution and continued through the mid-nineteenth century.

Each brick building was and continues to be a pivotal community symbol. The unadorned Counting House was built with a gambrel roof at the head of Straight Wharf by merchant William Rotch Sr. (1734–1828). The structure was used partly as his office, and the remaining space was occupied by the town, which had given Rotch the building site. Interestingly, this building is associated with an important event in American history. In 1773 the ships *Beaver* (owned by William Rotch) and *Dartmouth* (owned by William's father, Joseph Rotch) were sent to London with whale oil. Upon their return to Boston with English tea, the *Beaver* and *Dartmouth* were two of the three ships involved in the infamous Boston Tea Party.[1]

Consisting of brick and brownstone, with a gable roof and double chimneys, the Rotch Counting House is a singular example of Georgian-style commercial buildings, such as those built in Boston. A third story was added after the Great Fire of 1846. In 1860, seven whaling masters—the captains Samuel W. Wyer, George Palmer, Obed Swain, William S. Chadwick, Charles A. Veeder, James Wyer, and Samuel Swain—purchased the Rotch Counting House for use as a gathering place. They named it the Pacific Club,[2] following the precedent of the Pacific Bank, to pay homage to the

Pacific Ocean, its fabulously prolific whaling fields, and the island's resultant prosperity. Until recently, Pacific Club members and guests used the first-floor offices as a social club.

At the turn of the nineteenth century, the thriving Nantucket Town's street development continued, with scores of houses built and numerous public and commercial buildings erected to address the needs of the expanding whaling industry. The harmonious streetscape we admire today was at that time based on tradition, practicality, order, and good planning. Subdivision of land, street and alley layout, and individual lot dimensions were systematic, but sympathetic to existing landscape contours and the community needs, generally separating industrial and commercial areas from domestic activities. Following the Quaker custom of separating public and private space, lots were sited close to, often within five feet of, the public path, with the edge of the lot prescribed by fencing. Interior space was further defined: formal parlors used for socializing were located in the front of the house, while private family areas—the keeping room, kitchen, and chambers—were in the back, closer to the garden.

Joseph Starbuck's house, built at 4 New Dollar Lane (FIGURE 2) in 1809, represents the significant religious, cultural, and architectural changes taking place on Nantucket in the first decade of the nineteenth century. In fact, this book's study of six of the Starbuck family homes, beginning with the Christopher Starbuck House (circa 1690) in Chapter 1, chronicles Nantucket's architectural and cultural history from the very successful perspective of one of the island's first families. Each of the

{ ABOVE LEFT }
FIGURE 2: Joseph Starbuck House, Built in 1809, 4 New Dollar Lane (Twentieth-Century Addition on Right).

{ ABOVE RIGHT }
FIGURE 3: John Bisbee, Portrait of Joseph Starbuck, 1847. Collection of Mrs. H. Crowell Freeman.

{ ABOVE LEFT }
FIGURE 4: The Three Bricks, Built on Main Street, 1836–38, for Joseph Starbuck's sons.

{ ABOVE RIGHT }
FIGURE 5: Brick Federal-Style Gables, Main Street, as Seen from Liberty Street. Illustration by Rose Gonnella, 1995. Pencil on paper.

Starbuck homes is instructive. In his book *A Mirror of Nantucket,* George Allen Fowlkes describes Joseph Starbuck (1774–1861) and his 4 New Dollar Lane home: "When he married Sally Gardner, he was disowned by the Quaker meeting, for Sally's family belonged to the world's people. Therefore, it seemed quite natural to the practical-minded Starbuck to build a house in the same fashion as the more elaborate ones in town...."[3] There were several post-1776 residences that departed from the customary Quaker house type and were considered "elaborate" at that time, and are now defined as Federal style. These homes, including the Cary House at 117 Main Street, built circa 1800, and the 1800 Obed Macy House at 15 Pleasant Street, featuring symmetrical, double chimneys, open staircases, and wide halls extending from front to rear, most likely set the precedent for Joseph Starbuck's house plans.

Joseph and Sally Starbuck's house had fine paneling, wide floorboards, and a full brick basement with a cooking fireplace, unlike the house Joseph had been born in at 11 Milk Street. After initially working as a butcher, Joseph became a whaling merchant and whaleship owner. By 1852, Joseph's wealth was valued at $150,000, and he was considered one of the Commonwealth's richest men.[4] East of the house at 4 New Dollar Lane, he built the Joseph Starbuck and Company spermaceti candle factory (now a residence) and oil-house-try-works, since demolished. The Starbuck property then included what is now Starbuck Court, off Pleasant Street. The accumulated wealth was given to his family in the form of homes. Between 1836 and 1838 he had the identical East, Middle, and West

FIGURE 6: Unitarian Universalist Church, Built in 1809, 11 Orange Street (Also Known as South Tower and Second Congregational Meeting House).

FIGURE 7: Double Doors,
Unitarian Church, with
Blind Fan Ornament in
Greek Revival Door
Surround. Illustration by
Richard Valdes, 2003.

Bricks (FIGURE 4), as they are called today, constructed at 93, 95, and 97 Main Street for his sons William, Matthew, and George. These houses—imposing, five-bayed, classical, brick, center-entry masses, with stepped parapet end walls, square cupolas, and granite basements and steps—are regarded stylistically as transitional Federal-Greek Revival. In relation to the highly stylized classical designs being produced on the mainland at the time, these buildings reinforce the cultural restraint and time lag of architectural design on Nantucket, partly explained by the island's geographic isolation.

In the same year that Joseph Starbuck built the house at 4 New Dollar Lane, the present-day Unitarian Universalist Church at 11 Orange Street (FIGURE 6) was constructed as the Second Congregational Meeting House in 1809. Built by Elisha Ramsdell, the Orange Street church was erected in the Federal style, but there is no pictorial record of the original design.[5] Historian Alexander Starbuck tells the story of the church's bell and how it came to Nantucket: "The bell with its remarkably silvery tones, which has charmed so many, was not added until 1815. It was purchased in Lisbon by Capt. Charles Clisby and brought to Nantucket in 1812 on the schooner *William and Nancy*, by Capt. Thomas Cary. It was one of a chime of six, designed for a convent, but had not been consecrated. It was purchased for the Unitarian Church in 1815."[6] The first town clock was installed in the tower in 1823. The 1809 square tower, however, was not designed to sustain the weighty bell, and by 1830, oak beams were added for support and strength.

In 1844, the Unitarian congregation hired architect Frederick Brown Coleman to remodel the church's interior and exterior with classical elements. He designed the north and south facades' elegant windows, curved vestibule stairs, and decorative painting in the nave, executed by Carl Wendte, a Swiss artist who trained in Italy. The hierarchy of the symmetrical composition creates a compelling visual landmark, from the massive hand-carved blind fanlight above welcoming double doors (FIGURE 7), to the tower's orderly windows, elliptical decorative window, clock, and gold-domed lantern and weathervane. The church's simplicity of form and proportional beauty represents Nantucket's architectural aesthetic perfectly.

Forty-three years after the Rotch Counting House was built, the Pacific Bank (FIGURE 8) was erected in 1818, which, with its Federal-style geometry and curving forms, represented a far more refined aesthetic. In fact, architectural historian Clay Lancaster recognized the building as "the finest example of pure Federal-style architecture in Nantucket."[7] A compelling focal point at the top of Main Street, the elegant two-story brick and brownstone facade with colonnaded Roman Ionic portico, and fanlight-defined entry, is further emphasized by flared brownstone steps, a granite foundation, and first-story round-top window panels. Following the custom requiring banking staff to live close to their business, the rear part of the building was designed as a residence. William Mitchell

(1791–1869), astronomer, farmer, and the Pacific Bank cashier from 1837 to 1861, lived in the bank with his family. It was from the bank's rooftop observatory in 1847 that his daughter Maria (1818–1889) discovered a comet that distinguished her forever; she later became the first woman invited into the American Academy of Arts and Sciences, and a professor at Vassar College. Her legacy continues on Nantucket today through the Maria Mitchell Association.

Just as Thomas Jefferson had been inspired by the interpretative aesthetics of newly discovered classical Roman antiquities in France, in the nineteenth century the United States found inspiration from ancient Greece. British archeologists James Stuart and Nicholas Revett were the first scholars to document the monuments and temples of ancient Greece in their widely published work, *The Antiquities of Ancient Athens* (1762–1816). Across the emerging American states, these drawings were the source for practical design guides known as builders' companions. After the Greeks won the 1820 War of Independence from Turkey, American admiration for the Greek ideals of freedom and culture was unwavering. Initial late-eighteenth-century enthusiasm for the heavy-handed grandeur of Roman extravagance gave way to the order and simplicity of Greek temples.

The new national style spread from the colonial east to the Wild West, as entire new communities, houses, and public structures were built. Town squares and greens, High and Main streets all acquired temple-like, monumental public buildings of stone and masonry; in hamlets and villages, interpretations were made of wood and painted white, cream, and ochre to resemble those permanent materials of antiquity. State capitols, banks, churches, courthouses, schools, and libraries were surrounded with collections of white-painted frame houses that were smaller versions of the temple form.

With the rest of the nation, Nantucket hung up its humble gray colonial dress. The pre-Revolutionary remote island's Quaker-based way of life was transformed by its economic success in whaling and its introduction to foreign culture. Exuberant public buildings and residential applications of classical massing, form, and details remain throughout the

{ OPPOSITE }
FIGURE 8: Pacific Bank, Built in 1818, and the Methodist Church, Both Survivors of the Great Fire in 1846.

Town of Nantucket, reminders of Nantucket's relationship with the national, cultural, political, and social consciousness of self-governance in the first half of the nineteenth century. Islanders took up the new fashion, but tempered it with the island's inherent Quaker aesthetic restraint, "using the traditional four-bay forms and typical roof pitches with innovative Greek details."[8]

Frederick Brown Coleman is thought to have been responsible for the transformation of the Methodist church into a Greek temple. When built on Centre Street, in 1822–23, the church was an unremarkable wood building with a hip roof. Incredibly, the original hip roof remains intact under the massive 1840 timber-framed gable roof. The vast attic-story space created by the new roof profile is crisscrossed with huge twelve-by-twelve ship timbers up to sixty feet long, held together with traditional wood mortise-and-tenon joinery,[9] a testament to the outstanding skills of Nantucket shipbuilders and housewrights. Coleman's 1840 redesign resulted in a full-blown Greek Revival Ionic portico with six columns (FIGURE 9) under a full entablature and street-facing pediment. Unlike the Unitarian church, which is entirely shingled and painted white, the street facade of the Methodist church was covered in flush boarding, while the side and rear elevations were shingled and left to weather. Significant interior alterations in 1840 included shifting the orientation of the altar from east to west, creating balcony seating, and adding new pews designed with a slight raise in grade, to provide the congregation with visual access to the front of the church.

During this period, many of the hearth-centered, earth-bound early houses that derived from the rural medieval building tradition, and those that the Quakers developed as the typical Nantucket house, were fitted with the new style. Door surrounds were expanded with sidelights, toplights, and heavy pilasters; decorative interpretations of classic window trim included splayed lintels (sometimes still called "rabbit ears" on island); and "bull-nose," or half-round, molding that replaced early plank frames. Frequently, in the interest of thrift, builders/owners only had the public facade updated. In addition, center chimneys were removed and replaced by symmetrical end chimneys, to increase interior living spaces

FIGURE 9: Detail of the Methodist Church, Built 1822–23, Renovated 1840, Centre Street. *Recent restoration of the columns revealed their construction was similar to that used in making barrels.*

{ ABOVE }

FIGURE 10: Nathaniel Hussey Homestead, Built in 1753, 5 Quince Street. *Preservation restrictions provide for the protection of this home's historic interior and exterior elements in perpetuity.* Photograph by Jeffrey Allen.

{ LEFT }

FIGURE 11: J. Eastman Johnson, Portrait of Robert Ratliff, 1879. Oil on canvas. *The epitaph on Robert Ratliff's gravestone in the Old North Cemetery reads: "Honored for his integrity, respected for his uniform courtesy, and beloved for his kindness and generosity."* Courtesy of the Nantucket Historical Association. Gift of Eastman Johnson, 00.134.1

and open center halls, thus making room for gracious stairwells. In some cases, houses were raised above grade to accommodate basement and domestic activities, thus removing cooking heat and odors from living areas. Rough, unfinished, and colored surfaces were painted white to create the look of gleaming, ancient, carved, and chiseled stone.

The Nathaniel Hussey homestead at 5 Quince Street (FIGURE 10) was built by carpenter David Hussey in 1753 as a typical, timber-framed, center-chimney lean-to. An investigation of the attic revealed that the original center chimney was removed and an end chimney added. The house was then expanded to its present two-and-a-half-story, side-gabled, five-bay proportion. At the same time, the street-side windows and front entry were altered with classical details.

The changes most likely took place during the time British master rigger Robert Ratliff (1794–1882) occupied the house in the nineteenth century. Ratliff (FIGURE 11) was a seaman on the British ship *Northumberland*, which brought Napoleon Bonaparte to St. Helena in 1815. In 1820 Ratliff was shipwrecked on Nantucket, which remained his home until his death.[10] The house was further distinguished with architectural modifications made by its twentieth-century occupants, including Austin Strong (1881–1952), who first came to Nantucket in 1903 with his fiancée, Mary Holbrook Wilson. Strong was the step-grandson of Robert Louis Stevenson and was known on Nantucket as a successful New York playwright and artist, and for his association with the Nantucket Yacht Club as commodore and as the creator of the Rainbow Fleet. After purchasing the house in 1913, the Strongs added twentieth-century amenities, including finely crafted built-in closets, bookshelves, and bathrooms, while leaving the original eighteenth-century timber frame, hand-beaded beams, mitered gunstock posts,[11] and nineteenth-century classical details intact.[12]

Adapting to, and adopting, the Greek Revival style did not demand a completely new island building culture. Many of the components of the classic vocabulary—simplicity, order, restraint, and craftsmanship—related to Nantucket's Quaker building tradition. The most striking departure from Quaker architecture is easily described. Instead of facing the side of each lot, the roof gable was turned to face the street (FIGURE 12). The second and perhaps more obvious difference is the application of decorative classical elements. The facade of the house is topped by a triangular element, or pediment, in the attic-story gable, usually defined by heavily layered trim boards, and typically containing a decorative geometric or elliptical window. Entries became important visually, some because they were reached by stairs (the building was raised above grade level on a high basement), and also because great attention was given to finely carved detailing of door surrounds, porches, and columns. Corner pilasters framing the facade further defined the composition.

Recessed entries of Greek Revival homes were finished with elegant paneling (FIGURE 13) and corner quoins were carved to look like chiseled stonework. Geometric frieze and cornice decoration

{ OPPOSITE }

FIGURE 12: Facade, 6 Pine Street. *We see here the simplicity of a 19th-century Greek Revival cottage in the Fish Lots.*

{ ABOVE }

FIGURE 13: Recessed Entry, 21 Federal Street, with Paneling and Details Equal to Interior Finish Work.

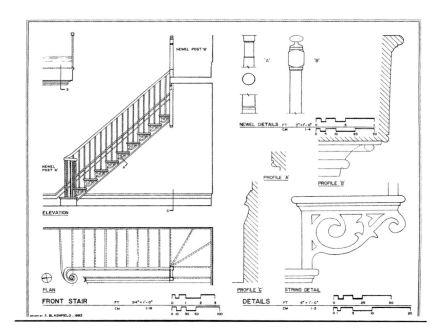

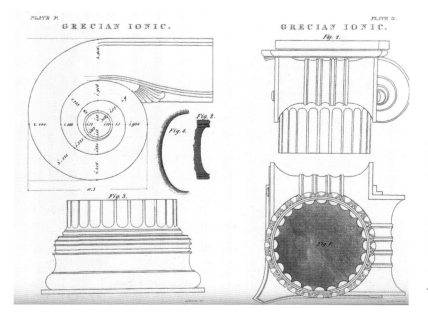

{ TOP }
FIGURE 14: Stairway at 22 Hussey Street, Dating to 1836. Illustration by Steve Blashfield. *Detailed carving on the stair risers was uniquely applied by Nantucket's wood-carvers.*

{ BOTTOM }
FIGURE 15: Grecian Ionic Column Detail. *From Asher Benjamin*, The American Builder's Companion *(1827, New York: Dover Publications, Inc., reprinted in 1969). Precise geometric forms that guided America's carpenters were found in builder's companions.*

on the facade included the "Greek key," dentil, swirl, volute, fillet, flute, and egg-and-dart patterns that were skillfully interpreted by Nantucket's housewrights. Interior details were equally elegant, as seen in the elevation and detail drawing of the front stair of the house built by William Andrews in 1836 at 22 Hussey Street (FIGURE 14).

Nantucket's conservative "shipbuilder-carpenter-contractor-architect"[13] depended on illustrated pattern books for inspiration and direction. Asher Benjamin's 1827 *The American Builder's Companion, or, a System of Architecture Particularly Adapted to the Present Style of Building*, was a primary resource in spreading classic design principles throughout the United States in the nineteenth century.[14] The popular book made available precise formulas and beautifully drawn designs, patterns, and details (FIGURE 15). Comparing the more elaborate Roman Doric aesthetic to the Grecian, Asher Benjamin writes, "the boldness of the Grecian Doric attracts the attention of the spectator by the grandeur and fine proportion of its parts, the form of its mouldings, and the beautiful variety of light and shade on their surfaces, which greatly relieves them from each other, and renders their contour distinct to the eye."[15] A footnote advises, "The small parts of every object ought to appear distinct to the eye at a reasonable distance from the building; for if this be not the case, it will be labour in vain, and will greatly diminish the beauty of the building."[16] Abundant examples throughout Nantucket Town prove that Asher's advice was followed, with local interpretation.[17]

Housewright Henry Macy built the handsome William H. Crosby house at 1 Pleasant Street in 1837 (FIGURE 16). Crosby (1815–1896) came to Nantucket from Boston to be a whale oil merchant. He was twenty years old when he married Elizabeth Pinkham, daughter of Nantucket whaleship Captain Seth Pinkham, on Christmas Day, in 1834. Crosby's financial position and sophisticated urbanity are reflected in the elegant design of his house, skillfully executed by a descendant of one of Nantucket's original founding families. At 1 Pleasant Street the Greek Revival style's cool geometric formality, strict use of proportion and order, and highly finished, almost polished, materials display a sharp contrast to the comfortably weathered Quaker houses that were built before the first half of the nineteenth century.

FIGURE 16: William H. Crosby House, Built in 1837, 1 Pleasant Street. *The Greek Revival style, with Boston influence, is evident in this building.*

Nantucket's Greek Revival houses, like 1 Pleasant Street, display endlessly exuberant variations of classic decorative elements. Greek key-patterned door surrounds; hefty columns topped with hand-carved volutes; small blocks of wood, called dentils, underlining an attic story; and wood quoins scored to look like blocks of stone survive on beautifully proportioned elevations. The architectural vocabulary is rich, and once learned, rewards the viewer with new discoveries all around Nantucket Town and in outlying areas, including on tiny Tuckernuck Island, where several cupola-topped farmhouses were built before the Civil War.

The style's most significant departure from earlier house types is dramatic. As mentioned previously, instead of gable ends facing the side yard, stretching the house across its lot, focusing on horizontal massing and lines, the narrow gable end faces directly on the street. Now, imitating the temple, verticality is emphasized. A good example of this style can be seen at 1 Pleasant Street (FIGURE 16), where soaring colossal-order pilasters rise above a high brick basement to visually support a pediment with a fan window in an elliptical outside frame. Topping off the two-and-a-half-story yellow clap-

FIGURE 17: Greek Key Pattern in the Window Frame, 1 Pleasant Street.

board facade is a square belvedere (from the Italian "fine view") best seen from Summer Street, as it is set back on the ridge of the slate roof. Enclosed belvederes and cupolas were typical during this period, replacing the early island practice of exposed, primitive walks—just one of the many features in the architectural evolution from the purely functional to highly decorative design elements influenced by classical forms.

On the left side of the thirty-foot-wide facade at 1 Pleasant Street, granite stairs set directly on the sidewalk are graced by a curved iron railing (an extension of the wrought-iron fence that defined the public sidewalk from private space). The steps lead up to a portico entry, framed by two fluted Doric columns supporting a decorative balustrade. Sidelights flank the paneled front door. The house originally included a very uncharacteristic, urban feature for Nantucket: an iron balcony across the front windows.

All the windows at 1 Pleasant Street are detailed with the Greek key, also known as the "meander pattern," in the upper head casing (FIGURE 17). The first-story double parlors' floor-to-ceiling triple-hung windows are also unique on Nantucket, an innovation known from Thomas Jefferson's house drawings, and can be seen at his own beloved Monticello. The second story's three bays hold six-over-six paned windows, protected from wind and rain by dark green or black shutters, also called blinds, introduced early in the nineteenth century on Nantucket.

The interior plan of 1 Pleasant Street is that of a formal city house, with dining room and kitchen located in the fenestrated basement. Nineteenth-century appreciation for the classical and aesthetic use of space is realized in the luxurious entry hall with a graceful three-story open stairwell. Records and letters from the time describe the twin parlors with marble mantelpieces on the first floor frequently filled with festive gatherings, including one at which frozen mousse was served for the first time on the island. Unfortunately, in addition to the loss of one whaling ship, and several other Crosby ships' poor voyages, the young family's financial stability finally crumbled when their warehouse, filled with oil, burned to the ground in Nantucket's Great Fire in 1846. A decade after the young family moved to 1 Pleasant Street, they were forced to sell the house.

The Crosby house design was undoubtedly taken from 54 Orange Street, built for Henry Field two years earlier, circa 1835, by house carpenter William Macy. Field owned a foundry in Providence that furnished the copper nails used in this construction. The Orange Street house is simpler in detail and execution, having no cupola and less ornate window frames.

One Pleasant Street follows the character and tradition of Nantucket buildings. The house remains simple and restrained, and it takes its place on the street without overt ostentation, despite its elevated foundation, innovative plan, and fine classical details. Compare the Crosby House to those houses built by William Hadwen (1791–1862), with backyards just across the street. Hadwen resided at 96 Main Street and built 94 Main Street for his wife's niece, Mary (Swain) Wright, whom he had adopted. Nantucket's most elaborate Greek Revival statements, sometimes called the "Two Greeks" (FIGURE 18), these mansions were designed by Frederick Brown Coleman and constructed circa 1844–45. Both display a cultural sophistication that Hadwen brought to Nantucket from his Newport, Rhode Island, background. While compelling in form and execution of detail, the "Two Greeks" depart from Nantucket's typically restrained response to mainland architectural influences.

Charming variations of one-, one-and-a-half-, and one-and-three-quarter-story Greek Revival cottages are sprinkled throughout the area known as the "Fish Lots," which once stretched from Union Street to Pine Street. In 1717, the area was subdivided for house lots, having first been used for drying codfish on wood racks, thus its name. Once it was subdivided, Quaker families built houses, shops, sheds, barns, necessaries, and other outbuildings behind the dwelling. Rough board fences contained the family's pigs and chickens.

At the corner of Pine and Darling streets stands a charming cottage (FIGURE 19). A high degree of craftsmanship and creativity resulted in this smaller version of a Greek Revival house type. Characteristic six-over-six windows are appropriately scaled to be smaller on these cottages, with half-round trim, also called "bull-nose" molding, and splayed lintels, or "rabbit ears," for the upper head casing. Front-facing pediments are

{ ABOVE }
FIGURE 18: "The Two Greeks," High Style Classical Residences at 94 and 96 Main Street, Built ca. 1844–45. Courtesy of the Nantucket Historical Association.

{ OPPOSITE }
FIGURE 19: Greek Revival Cottage at the Corner of Pine and Darling Streets, One of Two Similar Houses on Darling.

heavily trimmed out, with wide entablature and rake boards, and are always painted white.

The individual expression and expertise of the Nantucket housewright combined interpretations of Greek elements with strong maritime influences. At 26 Pine Street the distinctive wood stars applied to the facade came from the steam-sail Civil War battleship *Lancaster.*[18]

Respected architectural historian Clay Lancaster (1917–2000) described Captain Levi Starbuck's (1769–1849) house at 14 Orange Street as the "most masculine residence in Nantucket."[19] Indeed, every aspect of the house—elevation, plan, massing, facade, and detail—exhibits geometrical solidity and strength (FIGURE 20). Housewright William M. Andrews was twenty-seven years old in 1836 when he purchased the Orange Street site for $1,850. Earlier that year Andrews had completed 22 Hussey Street (FIGURE 21). It is interesting to contrast the two structures' main facades: both have gable ends facing the street, and are set directly on the public right-of-way. The 22 Hussey Street house is decorated with a variety of delicate classical details applied to a three-bay facade set directly on grade. The width and height of the house and the off-center placement of the front entry relate to earlier Nantucket Quaker house types. However, the strict symmetry of the Levi Starbuck house is a more confident Greek Revival design. Appropriately lifted above grade by an added basement level, and with the main entry facing south, the street facade becomes monumental, a truer temple interpretation. Pedestrian-scaled elements including window boxes and an elegant fence design soften the effect. When you consider the simple classical details of the Starbuck house, including Doric pilasters, fluted Ionic columns, Greek key pattern, and the exterior's cream and white palette, it is no wonder that the structure is one of Nantucket's finest examples of Greek Revival architecture.

The interior of the Levi Starbuck house is equally distinctive. The entry opens onto a curving, two-story, elegantly designed stair hall, which is ingeniously lighted by an oculus in the attic floor, under a roof skylight. An unusually elaborate grapevine design plaster cornice (FIGURE 22) in the double front parlor is based on an English pattern book discovered in the attic.[20]

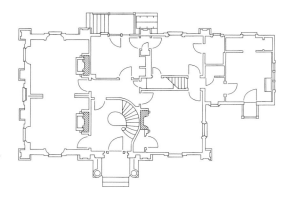

{ OPPOSITE AND ABOVE }

FIGURE 20: Captain Levi Starbuck House, Built in 1836, 14 Orange Street. *At one time 134 whaling captains lived on Orange Street.* Illustration by Branislav Bogdanovic, 2003.

{ OPPOSITE }
FIGURE 21: 22 Hussey Street, Built by Nantucket Housewright William M. Andrews in 1835.

{ ABOVE }
FIGURE 22: Grapevine Plaster Cornice Design, Levi Starbuck House.

Historic streets and neighborhoods are often associated with the community's social hierarchy. Orange Street was, and still is, known as the street where, over time, 134 wealthy sea captains once lived.[21] The idea that housewright William Andrews built 14 Orange Street as a speculative venture conflicts with public notices placed in the October 10 and 17, 1838, editions of the *Nantucket Mirror*, the first declaring Andrews's insolvency and the second, submitted by Andrews, stating that 14 Orange Street had "been intended for his own family residence. . . . Persons desirous of procuring a valuable and commodious dwelling can obtain a bargain in the premises by applying early to WM M ANDREWS."[22] Master mariner and Captain James Codd bought the house at 14 Orange Street from the heirs of Levi Starbuck in 1854. The price was $2,200, less than half its worth in 1838, indicating Nantucket's severe economic decline following the demise of the whaling industry. Subsequent owners have continued the remarkable care shown at 14 Orange Street throughout its history, so that this house truly retains the aura of oldness, the worn patina of many seasons, and the marks of hand tools on original wood members.

A history of the First Congregational Church (FIGURE 23) begins with the North Shore Meeting House, described by Alexander Starbuck as having been "removed from its original location near No Bottom Pond to Beacon Hill" in 1765. The building that was moved in 1765 is now called North Vestry and is the oldest continuing house of worship on Nantucket, still used for winter services and weddings. Beacon Hill is now called Academy Hill. The first Congregational Meeting House was built in Sherburne circa 1725, some sixty years after the island was settled by nonconformists who rejected the primacy of the Puritan ethos in the Massachusetts Bay Colony and had no interest in establishing an organized church. The Quakers built their first house of worship in 1711, and before then held meetings in private houses such as the Nathaniel and Mary Starbuck homestead.[23]

When the new First Congregational Church structure was built in 1834, the North Shore Meeting House was moved to the back of the site (FIGURE 24). By then, the interior had been altered many times, but the original timber-frame construction remained exposed, and the building

{ OPPOSITE }

FIGURE 23: First Congregational Church, Designed by Samuel Waldron, Built in 1834. Photograph by Gregory Spaid.

{ ABOVE }

FIGURE 24: North Shore Meeting House, First Congregational Church, Built ca. 1725.

still provides important evidence of post-and-lintel, mortise-and-tenon joinery. A tower was added to the meeting house in 1795, and a one-thousand-pound bell installed in 1800, when the town voted to have the bell "rung at Sun rise in the morning, 12 at noon and 9 at night."[24] This tradition was taken up in 1849 by South Church (Unitarian) on Orange Street, where the bell rings each morning at seven instead of at sunrise, but maintains the noon and nine o'clock schedule, when it rings fifty-two times after the hour is struck.

The 1834 design by Boston housewright Samuel Waldron[25] for the main Congregational church was unlike any public building design on Nantucket before or since (FIGURE 23). Interpreting the stone cathedrals of medieval Gothic architecture in wood, Waldron introduced curving ornament, verticality, and an emphasis on fenestration to an island architecture more practiced in elementary rectangular shapes. Architectural historians Calder Loth and Julius Trousdale Sadler Jr. consider the church "an excellent illustration of the conflict between Carpenters Classic and Carpenters Gothic."[26] On the facade, the exotic ogee arch over the front door, pointed arch windows with tracery, and decorative panels with four-lobed clover forms are applied to a traditional church tower. In 1840 the church nave was enlarged by one bay, and four additional pointed arch windows were placed on the north and south walls. At the same time, the original high octagonal steeple was removed and replaced by four minarets at the corners of the stepped belfry. A helicopter positioned the present steeple in 1968, when the building's exterior and interior were restored. In the summer, many visitors climb the ninety-four steps to the tower room to enjoy the 360-degree view of the town.

More discreet Carpenter Gothic details were applied to Greek Revival houses in Nantucket Town. The 1840 George Wendell Macy house on Main Street (FIGURE 25) is one of less than a dozen Greek Revival houses that also have Gothic details. Steeply pitched roofs and pointed arches, some with tracery, distinguish three houses built after the Great Fire on Whalers Lane and North Water Street. Situated on upper Main Street, just beyond three typical Nantucket houses, the George Macy house had a front gabled entry that was moved to the side under an engaged portico with a single Ionic column. A steeply pitched Gothic dormer window, placed above a secondary entry in the back ell facing the street, introduces intriguing and charming detail. A nearly identical design was built seven years later at 17 Pleasant Street.[27] George Wendell Macy (?–1889) served with great honor in the Civil War, one of 213 army and 126 navy volunteers from Nantucket. In fact, Nantucket enthusiastically exceeded its recommended quota for recruits and was named one of the Commonwealth's "banner-towns."[28]

Nantucket's remarkable architectural record is most often characterized as Quaker, yet the core historic and commercial district is largely Greek Revival in style. In his book, *Greek Revival Architecture in America*, Talbot Hamlin wrote about the impact of the Greek Revival style in New

{ OPPOSITE }
FIGURE 25: George Wendell Macy House, Built in 1840. *This house is notable for its Greek Revival main massing and Gothic Revival dormer detail.*

England, and noted that "Nantucket is especially interesting as showing the ideal the town builders of these prosperous towns were seeking to realize."[29] Main Street's classic Greek Revival building designs of brick and brownstone insert a sophisticated urbanity to the surrounding settlement composed of hundreds of typical Quaker dwellings. The reason for this juxtaposition is based on a catastrophe. On July 13, 1846, thirty-six acres of the town burned to the ground in a wind-swept fire that began at Geary's Hat Store, on the south side of Main Street. Hundreds of wood buildings that had served as the whaling port's shops, warehouses, banks, and offices were destroyed. Samuel H. Jenks Jr. drew a map of the area destroyed by fire that depicts the extent of the community's devastating loss and provides a blueprint for the study of Greek Revival architecture on Nantucket.

At the time of the Great Fire, Nantucket was brimming with the riches derived from its successful leadership in the world's whaling industry. Four banks, including the Pacific, Manufacturers and Mechanics, Citizens, and Institution for Savings, were operating. A highly sophisticated and diverse community of ten thousand islanders included professional tradesmen, specialized craftsmen, business speculators, and shipping masters. Because there are no records identifying the master planner(s) involved in the rebuilding of the burned-out area, speculation is that Frederick Brown Coleman played a significant role in the reconstruction. Coleman's previous work on Nantucket included the Methodist Church (FIGURES 8, 9) redesign in 1840; the Baptist Church (FIGURE 26) designed the same year; and the redesign of the Second Congregational Meeting House (FIGURE 6) in 1844.

The community of ten thousand, equal to the island's population in 2003, wasted no time in borrowing on its equity in order to reconstruct the burned streets, wharves, and structures that were essential to its economic and social well-being. Coleman's design for the Atheneum library (FIGURE 27) was realized just six months after the fire, an astonishing accomplishment, reflective of the Atheneum's importance. The two hundred commercial, public, and private Greek Revival structures that continue to grace the town today reveal the commitment, resources, energy, and most of all, the spirit of rebirth that surely inspired islanders more than 150 years ago.

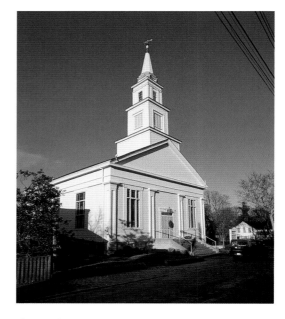

{ ABOVE }

FIGURE 26: Baptist Church, Designed by Frederick Brown Coleman, 1840.

{ OPPOSITE }

FIGURE 27: Atheneum, Designed by Frederick Brown Coleman, 1847. *The Atheneum library was the first building to be erected after the Great Fire of 1846.*

One particularly fine example of the Greek Revival style and the island's commitment to rebuilding the town is the Admiral Sir Isaac Coffin Lancasterian Schoolhouse, built in 1852–54 at 4 Winter Street (FIGURE 28).[30] Originally founded in 1827 by the Boston-born Englishman Sir Isaac Coffin, the school's second home was built for eight thousand dollars.[31] Constructed of brick, the building's elegant facade is distinguished by a series of marble steps leading up to a recessed portico framed by two white, fluted, Doric columns of wood. When designing the school, builders Benjamin Robinson, James Thompson, and Edward Easton[32] more than likely consulted Henry Barnard's 1848 pattern book *School Architecture*, which includes a facade design remarkably similar to the Coffin School.[33] Barnard recommended that schools be built in the Greek Revival style: "Every school house should be a temple, consecrated in prayer to the physical, intellectual, and moral culture of every child in the community, and be associated in every heart with the earliest and strongest impressions of truth, justice, patriotism and religion."[34] The building also reflects the taste of the wealthy trustees of the school, who lived in grand Federal-style and Greek Revival–style homes in town.

In spite of the heroic rebuilding of the business district after the Great Fire in 1846, a combination of nearly concurrent devastating events resulted in a deep economic depression that lasted until the 1870s. The discovery of first camphene, then lard oil, and finally kerosene removed the world's dependence on whale oil for lighting. In 1869, the *Oak* was the last whaleship to leave Nantucket Harbor.[35] The island's once-essential product was no longer needed. Beginning in 1849, more than five hundred men left Nantucket to seek fortunes in the California Gold Rush,[36] while more than forty-two whaleships were refitted to bring the adventurers around Cape Horn to California. The exodus, according to Alexander Starbuck, "carried away the bone and sinew of the Island and made a heavy draft on its recuperative energies."[37] Finally, the Soldiers and Sailors Monument on Upper Main Street reminds us that Nantucket lost seventy-three men who served in the Civil War.[38] Until Nantucket began to gain economic strength through the summer vacation industry in the mid- to late nineteenth century, the town's houses were reportedly abandoned. There were numerous newspaper reports of houses being moved off island—to Cape Cod, New Bedford, and even one house was taken by ship to Monterey, California. Moving buildings had been customary throughout New England and common on Nantucket since the closing of the harbor at Capaum.

It is true that Nantucket's architecture was kept safe by the historic episodes that began in 1846. Each event further diminished the town's vitality until its economy was completely depressed. Unlike other towns and cities that recovered and developed after the Civil War, as a result of the economic impact of the Industrial Revolution, Nantucket and its people were suspended, without the means to change or replace the old structures, our architectural inheritance.

{ OPPOSITE }

FIGURE 28: Admiral Sir Isaac Coffin Lancasterian School, Built in 1852–54, 4 Winter Street. *Despite an economic depression on the island, the trustees of the Admiral Sir Isaac Coffin Lancasterian School were able to build this magnificent schoolhouse in the popular Greek Revival style. The facade, with its dominant pediment and massive Doric columns, is modeled after a Greek temple.*

Restoration of the African Meeting House

JOHN A. JAMES

The African Meeting House on Nantucket, Built in mid-1820s.

THE AFRICAN MEETING HOUSE is an important reminder of the role African Americans played in the history of Nantucket and coastal New England. A study done by Nantucket teacher and historian Barbara Linebaugh indicates that the building, originally constructed in the mid-1820s, was initially built as a school and church. It served as a school for black children until Nantucket integrated its schools in the 1840s. The building continued to function as a meeting house through the end of the nineteenth century.

In the early twentieth century, the structure was sold by the congregation, which prompted its use for other purposes as well as its eventual deterioration. The building was saved by a few dedicated Nantucketers and eventually purchased in 1989 by the Museum of Afro American History in Boston. The following year the John A. James architectural firm was hired to begin the ambitious task of restoring the building as faithfully as possible. Matching grants from the Massachusetts Historical Commission facilitated the restoration, and the Society for the Preservation of New England Antiquities completed a Historical Structures Report.

This building represents a rare example of Nantucket architecture because of its hip roof and cove-shaped wall and ceiling. It is its spatial concept, and not its decoration, that dominates the interior, which consists of a single room of two materials, plaster and wood. The decorative treatment of the wood is limited to beading along the edges of the trim work and wainscoting. The finished floor is wide-board pine.

In restoring a structure that had so badly deteriorated and about which there was so little documentation, the architects relied heavily on the physical evidence of the building itself. There were portions of the flooring, wainscoting, plaster cove ceiling, casings of posts, and window sash that were preserved and used as models for replication. Although the entry facade had been removed and a rolling door installed, with the aid of a photograph dated 1880 in the collection of the Nantucket Historical Association, the team was able to design doors and windows that are very close to the original.

Further evidence that the entry facade had been modified over the decades was found. The earlier configuration showed a single door in the center and two windows of the size and position of the side windows. This was the original facade when the building first served as a school. The facade, as restored, with the double doors and high windows, and Greek key pattern over the doors (typical of the Greek Revival style) probably represents changes that were made when the building began to serve primarily as a meeting house, in the late 1840s or early 1850s.

For the interior, new pews were designed based on evidence from an imprint on the wainscoting and a pew door that was owned by the Historical Association. The pew "shadows" on the wainscoting and paint markings on the original floor provided the exact lengths and locations of the pews.

The goal for this project was to preserve and reuse as much of the original building fabric as possible. Where new construction was involved attempts were made to be faithful to the original materials and construction techniques. In the end the restored structure is in keeping with the original spirit, but usable for the new purposes defined by the Museum of Afro American History and the Friends of the Meeting House.

CHAPTER 4

Romantic Revivals:
Architecture for a Summer Resort Community

Margaret Moore Booker

*I*N the mid-nineteenth century, when the whaling industry had all but disappeared, the town of Nantucket looked desolate and deserted. The once thriving community of ten thousand had dwindled to merely four thousand people.[1] After visiting the island in 1866, one writer described it as "A little town, whose life stands still... whose ships have sailed away to other ports, whose inhabitants have followed... and whose houses seem to be going after the inhabitants."[2]

In the early 1870s, Nantucket emerged from decades of economic slump and made considerable strides in setting the stage for its future as a fashionable summer resort. As one guidebook from the period suggested, "Having furnished light for the world, [Nantucket] is now commencing to furnish health for the weary summer sojourner who lingers on her shore."[3] Although some small industries, such as farming, fishing, and the manufacturing of boots, shoes, and straw hats were undertaken, it provided islanders with a meager income. It became increasingly clear that the key to economic survival for a significant part of the population lay in promoting the island as a resort.

By 1874, express trains brought travelers from New York and Boston to Cape Cod, where two steamboats a day brought hundreds of passengers from the mainland to the island's shores. Visitors were attracted to Nantucket's cool ocean breezes, saltwater bathing, sailing, and other leisure activities. Travelers were also enchanted by the quaintness and romance of Nantucket's history as the former center of the global whaling industry. Historical landmarks, such as the Old Mill, Sankaty Lighthouse, and the Coffin School, were as popular with visitors as the sun and surf.

Contributing to the growth of the island's resort industry were illustrated articles touting Nantucket's attributes, published in popular periodicals such as *Harper's* and *Scribner's Monthly*, and the rise in wealth and leisure time, a result of the booming industrialization of nineteenth-century America. For the well-off, weekends and the summer months became times to escape the stresses of everyday life, as well as the heat and unhealthy air of the cities. They sought a simpler and healthier

{ OPPOSITE }

FIGURE 1: Eliza Starbuck Barney House, 73 Main Street, Built in 1872. *A host of eclectic styles were built during the Victorian era on Nantucket, including this example of the Second Empire style. The French-style roof, recessed entrance-way, heavy cornice brackets, and other details give the facade a three-dimensional sculptural quality.*

lifestyle at the seashore. In fact, the island advertised itself as a health resort. The *Inquirer and Mirror* claimed that after just a few "healthful" weeks on the island visitors returned to their homes with "a new lease of life, cheerful and happy."[4]

During the mid- to late-Victorian era[5] the island's culture was broadened and increasingly influenced by the summer residents, who introduced Nantucket to the latest in building fashions. The romance associated with the Victorian era and advances in building technology sparked a craze for architectural embellishment, leading to Gothic Revival, Queen Anne, Stick, and other romantic and eclectic forms, all of which were built on the East Coast and subsequently on Nantucket. The styles spread quickly, in part due to the publication of designs in both house pattern books and periodicals. On Nantucket, new homes built during this period were often the result of a builder's creativeness and skill, leading to inventive interpretations of mainland designs.

FIGURE 2: Eliza Starbuck Barney, ca.1875. *Described as "a central figure in Nantucket society—a leader in all literary and intellectual coteries," Eliza Barney needed a stylish home in which to entertain her guests and family, and to hold temperance and women's suffrage meetings. In her 73 Main Street house she also undertook the painstaking and important task of recording the island's genealogical history.* Courtesy of the Nantucket Historical Association.

The emergence of the romantic revival styles was part of the Picturesque movement in America, which brought a radical change to the shapes and plans of middle-class American homes.[6] Beginning with Gothic Revival, Americans broke free from the restraints of regularity, simplicity, and symmetry of forms dictated by earlier fashions and ideals. On Nantucket, as on the mainland, builders were encouraged to experiment, and the result was a new burst of creativity that led to irregular, asymmetrical exterior and interior shapes and arrangements. The asymmetry and variety of this Picturesque movement seemed to connote organic growth processes and freedom and originality—values prized in America at this time.[7] The change was also due in part to "balloon frame" construction, which became the preferred method of framing by the end of the century and made it possible to incorporate more complex architectural features, such as overhangs, bay windows, and towers.[8] In addition, new tools like the steam-powered scroll saw enabled carpenters to create the intricate and elaborate motifs of Victorian-period buildings.

One of the earliest examples of the new exuberant Victorian manner is the Eliza Starbuck Barney house at 73 Main Street (FIGURE 1). Remarkably, it was one of three large and elegant mansions built on Main Street in the early 1870s, when the island's economy was still at a low ebb and notices of homes for sale or to rent were posted on many "fine mansions and unpretentious houses all over the island."[9] These houses were the first substantial residences to be built in Nantucket Town in a quarter century.[10]

In the spring of 1872, three years after her husband died, Eliza Starbuck Barney (1802–1889) purchased land and a home on Main Street for five hundred dollars from Alice Swain. Barney (FIGURE 2) hired carpenters to dismantle the house, and had it replaced, as the *Inquirer and Mirror* reported, "by a new house, greatly to the improvement of the appearance of the street."[11] Built in the Second Empire style, the Barney home is distinguished by its mansard roof, heavy cornice withbrack-

FIGURE 3: Detail of the Door at 73 Main Street. *With its exquisitely carved wood and etched-glass panel, this door reflects the Victorians' belief that the first and most important impression made upon a visitor to a house was through its entranceway.*

brackets, wood cresting along the upper roofline, and elaborate cupola. The three bays, paired arched windows above the doorway, and the elaborately carved, paired entry doors (FIGURE 3) are also characteristic of the style.[12] Many villas and cottages were built in the Second Empire style in America between 1860 and 1880, and house designs similar to the Barney home can be found in pattern books of the era.[13]

Painted a vivid blue with bright white trim and gray accents,[14] the Barney home reflects the Victorians' "ever increasing demand for and love of color."[15] Numerous notices in the *Inquirer and Mirror* concerning new buildings or repainting indicate that it was not uncommon to find vivid colors on facades in Victorian Nantucket. For example, in June of 1878 it was noted that James M. Coffin and Son were painting the exterior of their store on Fair Street a "deep blue color," and several years later when additions were made to the Wauwinet House hotel they were painted in "fashionable dark colors."[16]

Restored in 1965, the elaborate facade of the Barney house was originally embellished even more, with finials topping the gables, arches, and cupola. The opulence of 73 Main Street is surprising considering that Eliza Barney, a temperance leader and abolitionist, had expressed distaste for "showy environments and useless luxuries" and was known for her "Quaker-like simplicity of living."[17] Barney's choice of house design may have been influenced by the grand villas built along the Hudson River, which she would have seen in the 1860s when she was living in the area,[18] or possibly by the house designs in *Godey's Lady's Book*, an influential magazine that promoted the French Second Empire style of architecture.[19] Eliza could certainly afford to build the elaborate mansion; she was the daughter of whaling industry tycoon Joseph Starbuck (1774–1861) and the wife of Nathaniel Barney (1792–1869), who along with his partner, William Hadwen, owned one of the island's most successful whale oil and candle businesses.[20]

Shortly after the Barney home was erected, the island's new-found tourism industry gave rise to rampant land speculation and building activity. The small seaside village of 'Sconset, at the eastern end of the island, became increasingly popular as the preferred summer resort area.[21] Builders and developers Charles H. Robinson (1829–1915) and Franklin A. Ellis (1833–1884) established the Sunset

Heights development in 'Sconset, below the junction of Main Street and Grand Avenue, in 1873. The favored style for the first seaside summer cottages and Ocean View House hotel of Sunset Heights was picturesque Gothic Revival. Fashionable in northeastern America from the 1840s to the mid-1870s, the style was inspired by medieval Europe and originated in England as a revolt against the rigid lines and symmetry of classic forms.

Tucked away on a quiet lane in 'Sconset, just a few short blocks from the ocean, Wolf's Head (FIGURE 4) is one of the few remaining Gothic Revival cottages of Sunset Heights. Built about 1873, it was more than likely designed by Charles Robinson and may have originally been part of the Ocean View House complex.[22] By the 1880s the cottage was known as

{ LEFT }

FIGURE 4: Wolf's Head, Built ca. 1873, 8 Cottage Avenue, 'Sconset. *This is one of the first cottages built by Charles Robinson at Sunset Heights in 'Sconset, in the Gothic Revival style.*

{ RIGHT }

FIGURE 5: Detail of Parapet, 8 Cottage Avenue. *Decorative wood details and pointed arch hoods over windows and doors are among the hallmarks of the Victorian Gothic Revival style.*

FIGURE 6: Charles H.
Robinson, ca. 1910.
*Responsible for building
most of the Victorian-style
homes on the island, Charles
H. Robinson remained an
active builder and astute
businessman well into his
eighties.* Courtesy of the
Nantucket Historical Association.

"Wolf's Head Inn"[23] and since 1921 has been owned by the Penrose family.[24] Characteristic of the Gothic Revival style, Wolf's Head has a steeply pitched roof with cross gables and pointed arches and drip-mold crowns over the slender windows and double front door. The fanciful carved wood railings, or "gingerbread," on the porch and second-floor parapet (FIGURE 5) are also common elements of the style. Early 1870s photographs of Sunset Heights' cottages indicate that the facade of Wolf's Head would have been further adorned with articulated vergeboards, pinnacles, and horizontal boarding.[25]

Wolf's Head is remarkably similar in style to the tiny, colorful two-story cottages that were built in the Methodist campground on Martha's Vineyard, Massachusetts, in the mid-nineteenth century.[26] It also recalls the earlier rural Gothic cottage designs of Andrew Jackson Downing (1815–1852), an influential American architect of the Gothic Revival style and a major trendsetter of his day. The front covered veranda, which became one of the hallmarks of mid- to late-nineteenth-century homes on Nantucket, was an important feature to Downing, who believed that no dwelling was complete without a porch or veranda, which served as a harmonious link between the house and the "picturesque" landscape in which it was situated. The subdued green color of the trim on Wolf's Head is also in keeping with Downing's taste, who was disdainful of white on house exteriors and recommended a "mellow hue harmonizing with the verdure of the country."[27]

According to family tradition, Wolf's Head was moved several times.[28] During much of the nineteenth century, as previously discussed, it was common to dismantle houses and reconstruct them elsewhere on the island, and even move them to the mainland.

The Gothic Revival style can be seen in Nantucket Town in the applied details of buildings, such as the sharply pointed arched windows at 6 Winter Street and 4 North Water Street. The Gothic Revival manner is fully realized in the magnificent facade of the 1834 First Congregational Church on Centre Street.

The exuberant nature of Victorian architecture can be seen in several buildings still existing in Nantucket Town. Most were erected by Charles H. Robinson (FIGURE 6), the island's most prolific architect/builder and contractor/realtor in late-nineteenth-century Nantucket. The son of builder Benjamin Robinson, Charles played a significant role in the growth of the island's resort industry. According to Clay Lancaster, when inclement weather kept Robinson indoors he spent long hours in his shop fabricating the lavish architectural embellishments that are characteristic of his style.[29] Two of his notable buildings extant today are at 21 and 19 Broad Street (FIGURE 7). The latter was built for island coal merchant Andrew Hunt[30] and displays the flaring mansard roof, bracketed eaves, bay window, and paired windows with scrolls typical of the French-inspired Second Empire style.[31] Robinson, like so many of his fellow island builders, consulted pattern books of the era in designing

{ OPPOSITE }
FIGURE 7: 19 Broad Street, Built in 1878. *The Victorian fondness for elaborately detailed roofs, porches, bay windows and a variety of color is evident in this home, built by Charles Robinson for island coal merchant Andrew Hunt.*

{ ABOVE LEFT }
FIGURE 8: Design No. 23, from E. C. Hussey's 1874 Pattern Book, *National Cottage Architecture* (New York: The American News Company, 1874; Dover Publications reprint, 1994). *Victorian-era builders often referred to pattern books for house designs; this one is similar to 19 Broad Street.*

{ ABOVE RIGHT }
FIGURE 9: 45 India Street, ca. 1890. *As we can see in this typical Nantucket house built ca. 1804, during the later nineteenth century many Nantucketers updated their homes by adding Victorian details such as porches, shingle patterns, dormer windows, hoods over doorways, and decorative trusses in the gables.* Courtesy of the Nantucket Historical Association.

his buildings, and 19 Broad Street resembles the published designs of American architect E. C. Hussey (FIGURE 8).[32]

In addition to erecting new structures, Robinson and other island carpenters and builders "modernized" many island homes in the mid- to late-nineteenth century with decorative features of the popular Victorian style. Elaborate wood details, such as gable vergeboards and pinnacles, ornamental hood moldings over doorways, pointed arched windows, or lacy second-floor parapets, as well as wide piazzas and bay windows, were superimposed over the plain, shingled facades of typical Nantucket-style homes, creating uniquely personal dwellings (FIGURE 9). In the early to mid-twentieth century, when this type of decoration was no longer popular, these houses were restored to their original designs and stripped of their fanciful details. Around the same time, several of the island's grand late-nineteenth-century hotels and residences were demolished. And thus, much of Victorian Nantucket disappeared.

There is a movement today among several historic preservationists to restore some of the island's former Victorian-era glory. Among them are Valerie and Richard Norton, of Norton Preservation Trust, whose

{ OPPOSITE }

FIGURE 10: 51 Fair Street. *Architectural pattern books contained only a handful of drawings of brackets and other decorative features, so local carpenters like Charles Robinson, who built this Victorian-style home in 1877–78, created their own fanciful designs.*

{ ABOVE }

FIGURE 11: Porch Support Detail, 51 Fair Street.

strong sense of tradition is evident in their painstaking restoration of the house at 51 Fair Street (FIGURE 10). Architect/builder Charles Robinson purchased the land for this house, originally a spec project, in October of 1877. He began building in December, sold the property to Nantucketer George E. Harris (1852–1918) in January of 1878, and completed the house for him in late February.[33]

Typical of Robinson's smaller homes, 51 Fair Street is a modest, simple house form with the decorative details confined to the porch, cornice line, and windows. Some of the embellishments, such as the pointed arch moldings over the prominent gable windows and bay window, are typical of the Gothic Revival style.[34] The porch has carefully re-created ornamental woodwork (FIGURE 11) that would have been constructed with a scroll saw by the builder.[35]

When restoring the exterior of 51 Fair Street, the Nortons scraped the paint layers to find the original hues; they chose the second layer: mustard for the clapboard and different shades of khaki for the trim. In keeping with Victorian tradition, the trim is darker than the main body of the house, and is complementary in tone. Among the original or first layer of trim colors at 51 Fair was a dark green and vivid turquoise. While this may seem surprising today, it was not unusual for Nantucket in the late 1870s and early 1880s. In fact some residents and summer homeowners took the Victorian love for color to an extreme, and red became the "artistic thing for seaside cottages."[36] These vivid colors shocked some Nantucketers, including schoolteacher Elma Folger, who complained in a letter to a friend: "The Johnsons have painted their house a deep red, and the window-sills and doors etc. yellow. The Nantucket people shake their heads and wonder what it all means, and what everything is going to."[37]

As the century progressed, the island's tourism grew into its heyday of large hotels, charming summer cottages, restaurants, and other centers catering to a rich and varied social life. The island's late Victorian era signaled a return of prosperity not seen on the island since the golden age of whaling. The year-round population remained only approximately three thousand, but by 1881 "ten thousand pilgrims" were drawn to visit the island each summer "to enjoy the elixir of health, the solemn

beauty of the ocean, the antiquity of the town, [to] converse with agreeable fellow beings, or...[for] complete retirement."[38]

The gloomy foreboding as to the future finally dissipated, and the town and smaller hamlets were brightening up in every way. Housepainters and builders experienced a thriving trade, roads were improved, and many new amenities were established for the tourist trade. For example, a single narrow-gauge railroad was begun in 1880, with extensions running to outposts at Surfside beach by 1881 and to Siasconset in 1884.

New construction shifted from Nantucket Town to more spacious sites along the seashore. The first area to be developed just outside of town was the "Cliff," a sandy bluff overlooking Nantucket Sound that was divided into lots in 1872. Among those to build a summer home there was the artist Eastman Johnson, in 1871, and New York lawyer Charles O'Connor, in 1881.[39] The next major area to be developed near town was Brant Point, beachfront property along the harbor that was originally called "Cliff shore" and later "Beachside."[40] In 1880 Edwin James Hulbert (1829–ca. 1910), a mining engineer from Middletown, Connecticut,[41] purchased a two-hundred-square-foot lot for two hundred dollars and the following year built the first Beachside home: a magnificent two-story Queen Anne–style edifice called "Sandanwede" (FIGURE 12).[42]

FIGURE 12: Sandanwede, Built in 1881, Hulbert Avenue. *The Nantucket* Inquirer and Mirror *reported in June of 1881 that Sandanwede, with its main facade facing the water, "is pleasantly located, commanding an unobstructed view of the sound and inner bay." The location was perfect for a Queen Anne–style home, as house pattern books of that era dictated that English-style cottages were intended for picturesque, rural locales, just like the unruly waterfront of Nantucket.* Courtesy of the Nantucket Historical Association.

FIGURE 13: Detail of Sandanwede, Hulbert Avenue. *Sandanwede is notable for its distinct sunburst-motif porch supports. The supports and trim were originally painted a warm, neutral color that complemented the facade and harmonized with nature. In the Victorian era white was considered too cold and glaring and was rarely used on exteriors.*

Fashionable in America in the 1880s and 1890s, especially along the northeast coast, the Queen Anne style was named and popularized by a group of nineteenth-century English architects, led by Norman Shaw, who drew upon late medieval models of architecture.[43] When Sandanwede was being constructed, the *Inquirer and Mirror* noted that the style of architecture was "the ancient English cottage pattern."[44] In fact, the design of Sandanwede reflects both the English influence and the house patterns of American proponents of the Queen Anne style, such as Eugene C. Gardner and Henry H. Holly.[45] The English Queen Anne influence can be seen in the variegated rooflines and gables, steeply pitched roof, and asymmetrical facade, while the distinctive American features are apparent in the shingle siding, spacious veranda, and compact design.

Other distinctly Queen Anne–style features of the house are the window sashes with many small square panes running along the edges, and the crisp, machine-turned spindles and sunburst brackets of the veranda (FIGURE 13). The latter exhibits the inspiration of Charles L. Eastlake (1836–1906), an English architect and interior designer whose furniture designs were transposed into a domestic building style distinguished by ornate carved and turned wooden decoration.[46] From the Eastlake-style veranda, the Hulberts enjoyed magnificent views of the ever-changing colors of the seawater, the gently sifting sands of Coatue, the steady stream of yachts and steamships entering the harbor, and at night the bright beams of light emanating from Brant Point lighthouse.

Nantucket-born James H. Gibbs (1822–1908), who became a successful builder and contractor on the island after his hopes for a fortune in the California Gold Rush were dashed, built Sandanwede.[47] Begun in the spring of 1881, the construction of the house caused quite a stir on the island. In May of 1881 a reporter for the *Inquirer and Mirror* noted that Gibbs had the "frames and trimmings" shipped from the mainland for the Hulbert home.[48] And one month later the newspaper reported that a "large force of workmen" was engaged in building the cottage, which "will be one of the handsomest residences in these parts."[49]

After building their summer cottage, Edwin Hulbert (FIGURE 14) and his wife, Frances, became prominent members of the summer island community, their comings and goings noted in the personal column of the *Inquirer and Mirror*.[50] The style of their home, suited to the lifestyle of summer resort areas, became popular on the island. For example, two years after the completion of Sandanwede a house was built on Brant Point for H. L. Breed in the Queen Anne style.[51]

The erecting of many Victorian summer "cottages" soon followed in Beachside and elsewhere on the island. The building of so many new structures in rural areas for holiday revelers disturbed some island residents. For example, in 1882 Elma Folger complained in a letter to a friend that a house was being built for the daughter of the editor of the *New York Sun*: "Someone is putting up a house over on Shimmo Hills.... [I]t's awful to see the houses going up so—I suppose it's the natural consequence—though."[52]

Another area that experienced an enormous building boom in the period was 'Sconset. A stroll along the path bordering the village's north bluff, with breathtaking vistas of the ocean, is perhaps the best vantage point from which to study the predominant architectural styles of the 1880s and 1890s. Second Empire, Queen Anne, Stick, Shingle, and Colonial Revival are all represented. When they were first built these homes were not well received by some islanders. In 1886 one 'Sconset resident observed, "Some of the new structures are modern and ornate in style, in strange contrast with the generally modest architecture of the island, and markedly so when compared with the 'Sconset cottages."[53] However, by this date it was common to find colorful and eclectic homes on the island; an advertisement for five homes for sale on Ocean Avenue in 'Sconset noted that "These house are all different in structure and painted in different colors to avoid a monotonous appearance."[54]

In the late nineteenth century a cliff-front house on the north bluff (also known as "The Bank") in 'Sconset was a highly sought-after commodity. The beautiful vistas of the ocean and moors, "healthful" breezes, the romantic lighthouse nearby, and "peace and restfulness" of the place made it attractive. One of the first homes built on the north bluff was "Idlemoor" (FIGURE 15) at 11 Baxter Road, built in 1884 as a summer retreat for Abraham W. Rice, a financial manager of the Detroit Safe Company in Detroit, Michigan.[55] His home was built on land originally subdivided by William J. Flagg,[56] and as with most of the houses on Baxter Road, it sits graciously on a spacious lawn with its facade facing the ocean.[57] At that time, grass lawns reflected the rise of genteel outdoor sports such as croquet, lawn tennis, and badminton.

FIGURE 14: Edwin J. Hulbert, ca. 1895. *A successful mining engineer from Middletown, Connecticut, Edwin J. Hulbert built the first summer home in Beachside, in the fashionable Queen Anne style. Today's Hulbert Avenue was named after him.* Courtesy of the Nantucket Historical Association.

FIGURE 15: Idlemoor, Built in 1884, 11 Baxter Road, 'Sconset. *Victorian architecture by nature is inventive and diverse in color and style, as can be seen in the rich blue color, fanciful trim, and decorative shingle work of Idlemoor. On a bright, sunny day, the vergeboards enliven the facade by creating a lively pattern of shadows across the surface.* Photograph by Gregory Spaid.

Little is known about the builders of Idlemoor, carpenters E. A. and M. B. Leighton, except that they were from Cottage City (now known as Oak Bluffs) on Martha's Vineyard. They were particularly active on Nantucket in the mid-1880s, and their projects were frequently reported in the local paper.[58] When Idlemoor was under construction the *Inquirer and Mirror* noted its progress: "The Messrs. Leighton have commenced work upon a house for Mr. A. W. Rice on his land north of the village."[59] When it was completed in April of 1885, the paper exclaimed that the "cottage house" was "pronounced a beauty by all who have seen it."[60] Rice was so pleased with the house that he contemplated spending the whole year there, rather than just the summer months.[61]

Named after the view of the moors from the third floor and the relaxing or "idle" nature of the Rice family's visits to the house, Idlemoor has been owned by the same family for eight generations.[62] Like many Victorian houses the structure is asymmetrical, with a steeply pitched gable roof, cross gables embracing a square gabled tower, and elongated windows that emphasize the verticality of the facade. It is also distinguished by overhanging eaves, multi-textured wall surfaces, and a pretty porch that wraps around three sides of the house. The overall style of the home is reminiscent of mail-order house plans published in the late 1870s and early 1880s, in particular those reproduced in *Palliser's American Cottage Homes* of 1878.[63]

Idlemoor is one of the finest examples on island of the Stick style. Another adaptation of medieval English building traditions, the style stresses the exterior wall surface as the decorative element.[64] The facade of Idlemoor is enlivened by many imaginative decorative details (FIGURE 16), including five different shapes of wood shingles,[65] articulated gable verge-boards, eave brackets, curved sunburst-pattern porch supports, and varied patterns created by the raised wood siding and diagonal, flat stickwork.

Much further along the bluff is a house known as "Mayflower" (FIG-URE 17). Built circa 1893–94 as strictly a summer cottage with no heat, it is one of the purest examples of the Shingle style on Nantucket. The exterior consists of a continuous sweep of wood shingles. Laid out in horizontal courses, the shingles cover the undulating surface of the roof, run down

FIGURE 16: Detail of Idlemoor. *The ample porch with sun-burst pattern supports extends the interior volume of the house and reflects a love of nature.* Photograph by Gregory Spaid.

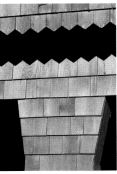

{ LEFT }

FIGURE 17: Mayflower, Built ca. 1893–94, Baxter Road, 'Sconset. *Typical of the Shingle style, the Mayflower's gable overhangs an expansive porch that provides welcome shade from the hot summer sun, a much needed commodity on the windswept, treeless bluff in 'Sconset.* Courtesy of the Nantucket Historical Association.

{ RIGHT }

FIGURE 18: Diamond-edged Shingles, Detail of Mayflower. *The shingle patterns of the Mayflower create a subtle play on the facade between light and shade, solid and void.*

the walls, and encircle the porch columns. The primary ornamentation on this stark exterior is found in the irregular textures of the weathered shingles and the crisp, diamond-shaped edging along the overhanging roofline (FIGURE 18). Also typical of the Shingle style is the broad, low-slung triangular gable, which is broken up on the street facade by a gambrel roof and on the bluff side by the balcony. The Mayflower does have a few playful details, such as the classical half-round windows on the end gables.

While some aspects of the Mayflower, like the shallow overhangs at the gable ends and the profusion of shingles, hearken back to seventeenth-century New England architecture, the overall style is distinctly modern. In sharp contrast to the ornate, highly ornamented Victorian homes on the island, the Shingle-style Mayflower is a building reduced to elemental form and stripped of extraneous detail. The beginning of modernism in

American architecture, the Shingle style appeared frequently in seaside architecture in coastal New England in the late 1800s.

The Mayflower is named after Mary "May" Wilson (1854–1899), who purchased the land in 1892. According to family tradition, her sister Clara (1857–1930) designed the six-bedroom house that was built on the site.[66] May was a teacher in Boston, and Clara was an artist and lecturer; both summered in 'Sconset beginning in the 1880s, along with the rest of their family from Washington, D.C.[67] Owned today by the grandnieces of May and Clara Wilson, the Mayflower has been beautifully preserved.

The interiors of Victorian cottages on the island were built with more open and free forms, with hallways, parlors, and wide doorways, as compared to the more rigid and box-like arrangement of rooms in most eighteenth- and early-nineteenth-century Nantucket homes. Much of the new flexibility was due to balloon frame building, as discussed earlier, and improvements in central heating; warmth was produced in the basement in a steam boiler or hot air furnace and distributed throughout the building.[68] Rooms no longer had to be compact and enclosed to retain the heat from the generous-sized hearth.

One of the few unblemished Victorian interiors on the island can be seen at 76 Main Street Inn, in Nantucket Town. It was originally constructed in 1887 for Captain William T. Swain (1835–1905), a native of New London, Connecticut, who hunted sea elephants and whales for a Nantucket company beginning in the 1850s.[69] Although the exterior of the house has been altered enormously in the last century, a rich variety of original architectural features can be found in the first-floor rooms and entryway (FIGURE 19). When Swain retired from the sea in 1876, he purchased a lumberyard on Nantucket and had access to the finest woods and woodworkers on the island.[70] The entrance contains the main stairway consisting of highly glossed handrails and turned balusters, and a prominent square newel post with applied wood carvings of a deer and foliate designs. The hall is further embellished by wood scroll brackets with incised and carved geometric and floral decoration (FIGURE 20), applied ornamental plasterwork molding on the ceiling, patterned hardwood floors; and wood wainscoting with carved wood tiles of floral designs (FIGURE 21).[71] The overall design of the hall is

{ OPPOSITE }

FIGURE 19: Entrance Hall at 76 Main Street, Built in 1887. *When this home was built for Captain William T. Swain, the owner was a leading builder on Nantucket and had access to the finest wood and woodworkers on the island, as is evident in the elaborate and finely crafted wood details of the entrance hallway.*

"Eastlake style," inspired by the influential English designer Charles L. Eastlake, who advocated three-foot-high wainscoting, ornate wood floor patterns, and simple, incised wood decoration.[72]

Victorians typically lavished much care in the design and decoration of the entrance, as it was the first "room" visitors encountered when entering the house. This space was treated as a symbol of the status and lifestyle of the residents. When he built his home, Swain was known on island as an "energetic and ambitious" businessman and builder, and was a prominent member of the Masonic lodge.

No longer the primary heating source, the fireplace in Victorian homes became much smaller and shallower, but retained its importance as a focal point of most rooms. A particularly appealing fireplace was built in the 1890s in what is now the Merrill home at 27 Hulburt Avenue (FIGURE 22). It features a curved brick opening, two terra-cotta inserts with foliate decoration (FIGURE 23), and wood bracket mantle supports with a lightly carved floral design.[73] The distinctly Romanesque Revival style of the fireplace was clearly inspired by the curved arched openings in the brick buildings designed by the influential Boston architect Henry Hobson Richardson (1838–1886), who spent at least one summer on the island and is known as the father of the Shingle style.[74] The Romanesque Revival style also made its appearance on the island in the heavy textured stonework and rounded arch entrance of St. Paul's Church on Fair Street, built in 1901, and in the rounded arch doorways of St. Mary's Church on Federal Street.

Whatever form they took, Victorian houses on Nantucket incorporated a wealth of varied styles and architectural influences. They were models of domestic comfort and in large part adapted for a summer tourist community that continued to grow. As the *Inquirer and Mirror* noted in 1899, "The demand for cottages is daily increasing, and the real estate men are busy as bees."[75]

{ TOP }
FIGURE 20: Wood Scroll Detail, Entrance Hall, 76 Main Street.

{ BOTTOM }
FIGURE 21: Applied Wood Floral Motif, Entrance Hall, 76 Main Street.

{ TOP }

FIGURE 22: Romanesque Revival–style Brick Fireplace, Merrill House, Built in the 1890s, Hulbert Avenue. *More than just a source for heat, the fireplace was the cornerstone of domestic life in Victorian homes, as well as the visual focus of the living room. This lovely curving fireplace has an added decorative feature: terra-cotta foliate inserts.*

{ BOTTOM }

FIGURE 23: Terra-cotta Tile, Merrill House Fireplace.

"The Embodiment of Quaintness":
Nantucket Architecture Lures Artists to the Island

MARGARET MOORE BOOKER

James Walter Folger, *Old Swain House, Polpis, 1672*, 1889. Oil on canvas. Egan Institute of Maritime Studies, Nantucket, Mass.

AS EARLY AS 1858 a correspondent for the art and literary magazine the *Crayon* exclaimed that on Nantucket Island "more subjects for pictures exist than artists to paint them!"[1] As the century progressed, artists with their portable easels, paint boxes, and white umbrellas became a common sight on the island in the summertime. By the early 1880s, the island was known as "an artists' retreat" where painters could find "many a nook and corner queer enough for their delicate brushes,"[2] and several notable American artists could be found summering in homes along Cliff Road.

To meet the increasing demand of a growing tourist market for souvenirs many artists chose to portray the island's architectural landmarks. Tourists were as enchanted by the quaintness and romance of Nantucket history and artifacts as they were by its cool ocean breezes, saltwater bathing, and other amenities.

In some instances, buildings were painted so frequently by artists that they became icons of the island's early history. Among them was the Swain farmhouse, built in the early eighteenth century (and destroyed by fire in 1902). A writer for the *Inquirer and Mirror* predicted the interest in the house: "If it proves that the George Swain house in Polpis is the oldest structure upon the island, what a perfect stampede of photographic and oil and water color artists there will be to Polpis in the summer of 1887."[3]

Indeed, the dilapidated, shingled Swain house with its "catslide" roof proved to be enormously appealing as a prized remnant of Nantucket's rural past. Among the artists who portrayed the farmhouse were island craftsman James W. Folger (1851–1918), Chicago watercolorist Jane B. Reid (1862–1966), Boston artist and teacher William N. Bartholomew (1822–1898), and noted island photographer Henry S. Wyer (1847–1920).

One of the more popular sketching destinations on Nantucket was the small village of Siasconset (called 'Sconset), located at the eastern end of the island. By 1880 the village's diminutive, often rambling and sometimes eccentric shingled houses—many of which were originally built in the 1700s by codfishermen—had been renovated into summer cottages. These tiny houses gained the distinction in the late nineteenth century as being the "embodiment of quaintness."[4] Artists Jane Reid and Lillian Gertrude Smith Rockwood (1863–1945) became known for their faithful, meticulous watercolor representations of the diminutive, rose-covered cottages of 'Sconset. Rockwood painted several versions of the picturesque Auld Lang Syne, on Broadway, possibly the oldest structure on the island, which served as her summer home and studio for decades.

While some artists painted accurate portraits of Nantucket's oldest buildings, others created more romantic, atmospheric visions. For example, around 1870, famed American genre painter Eastman Johnson (1824–1906) painted *The Quaint Old Village*, in which the surrounding landscape plays as important a role in the composition as the old buildings. In the 1880s Wendell Macy (1845–1913), a versatile artist and a descendant of one of Nantucket's earliest settlers, painted several idyllic sunset scenes of the "Old Sam Winslow House" on Quince Street. Annie Barker Folger (1852–1936) captured rural, turn-of-the-century Nantucket in her pastel streetscapes of run-down, shingled homes on sandy, winding roads.

By exhibiting their representations of Nantucket in art capitals across the country, artists helped the island gain distinction as a "famous watering-place." As Arthur E. Jenks noted in 1897, "[W]e cannot afford to be blind to what artists, local and foreign, are doing to bring Nantucket into prominence as a charming summer resort."[5] Today, works by these artists are treasured resources for anyone with an interest in studying the architectural history of Nantucket, and in some instances provide the only known images of some of the island's earliest architectural gems.

1. P., "Country Correspondence," *Crayon 5*, part 9 (September 1858), 270.
2. I&M, 5 August 1882.
3. I&M, 9 October 1886.
4. Edward F. Underhill, *'Sconset by the Sea* (Nantucket, Mass: Edward F. Underhill, 1893).
5. Arthur Elwell Jenks, "An Hour on 'Sconset Moors," I&M, 25 September 1897.

A View of SIASCONSET a Fishing Village on Nantucket.

{ CHAPTER *5* }

Fishermen's Shanties to Vacation Cottages:
The Architectural Evolution of Siasconset Village

Rose Gonnella

{ OPPOSITE }

FIGURE 1: A View of Siasconset, a Fishing Village on Nantucket (Engraving frontispiece to D. A. Leonard, *The Laws of Siasconset; A Ballad*, New Bedford, Mass., 1797). *'Sconset fishermen busy at their task and the village with its characteristic whale houses can be seen in this early engraving. At right, one house is under construction and the posts and beams, rafters, diagonal braces and window frames are depicted. When describing the village of 'Sconset, Edward Underhill noted: "Nearest land East, Portugal. Ditto South, the West Indies. Neither in sight. 200 houses big and little perched on a grassy bluff. Such is 'Sconset."* Courtesy of the Nantucket Historical Association.

*N*EXT stop, Portugal. Siasconset village, on the easternmost shore of Nantucket, is perched on a sandy bluff overlooking the vast Atlantic Ocean. Its inhabitants have benefited from and enjoyed access to an unobstructed and panoramic view of the wide rolling sea for well over three hundred years (FIGURE 1).

The English colonists of Nantucket, who originally came to the island with the intent of making their livelihood in the sheep and wool trade, quickly understood the more lucrative potential of the sea. With guidance from the native Wampanoag Indians, the settlers learned of the best fishing locations along the island's southern and eastern beaches.[1] They traveled from their northerly settlement at Sherburne to the farther reaches of the island to reap the fruits of the seemingly limitless ocean.[2] Its bounty was surely great. With cod, sea bass, smelt, perch, and pike to catch, it is said the people regarded the southeastern ocean as a great "stew pond."[3] In addition to fishing, the English inhabitants were also in pursuit of whales. The Wampanoags had been harvesting whales that had drifted close to shore and the English followed suit.

Recognizing the value of fishing and whaling as a means of both personal sustenance and as a livelihood, the English established in the 1660s and 1670s four seasonally occupied fishing stations along the southern and eastern shores of Nantucket, each equipped with rudimentary shelters for sleeping. Henry Forman, who has written a history of Siasconset and its fishing/whale houses, notes that by 1676, the Sesachacha station on the eastern shore had thirty cottages, making it the first English settlement of some size outside of Sherburne.[4] None of the fishermen's shanties of the southern stations or Sesachacha remain (FIGURE 2). As with the English dwellings of old Sherburne, many of the primitive dwellings were relocated to a more advantageous position along the shore. Over the course of many decades, shelters from Sesachacha were moved two and a half miles south along the thirty-foot-high Siasconset bluff, a strategic vantage point relative to the migration of whales.[5] Some cottages were also built on site.

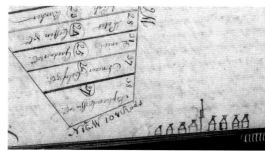

The strictly utilitarian fishing/whaling cottages were, at first, crude structures with only one room of post-and-beam construction and a symmetrical gable roof (FIGURE 3). They are related in design—although smaller in area and lower in height—to the English dwellings built by the seventeenth-century settlers at Capaum Harbor.[6] In addition, interior features (principally, a sleeping loft) were an adaptation from cottages known in fifteenth-century Wales.[7]

The small-scale whale cottages had a minimum of construction materials, heating, and maintenance needs. Fisherman obviously required the barest of shelters for their needs. Heating was not necessary because their use was during warmer months, and cooking was done outdoors or under a open shed, known on Nantucket as a porch.[8] Resident historian and grandson of a noted Nantucket carpenter, Obed Macy (1762–1844) wrote of the minimally constructed whaling huts in a journal entry of 1839: "Siasconset was formerly confined to the fishing business. The houses were buitl [sic] accordingly with wooden chimneys. The uprights not shingled,—and every calculation to make all the savings they could by fishing."[9]

By the mid-1700s, when the great harbor of Sherburne became the epicenter of a deep-sea whale fishery, near-shore whaling in 'Sconset waned. Codfishing, however, continued in earnest. Eventually, wives and

{ LEFT }

FIGURE 2: Fishing Shacks of Quidnet Village Near Seschacha Pond, ca. late 1800s. *These fishing shanties give a clue as to the style and random arrangement of shelters erected in earlier centuries elsewhere on the island.* Courtesy of the Nantucket Historical Association.

{ RIGHT }

FIGURE 3: Plot-Plan of Siasconset, 1775. *This schematic drawing delineates ownership of the house lots in Siasconset and depicts a row of cottages. Adjacent to the single room structures shown on the plan is a tall pole that was erected for a bird's-eye view of whales.* Photograph by James McIntosh. Registry of Deeds, Town of Nantucket, Massachusetts. Courtesy of the Egan Institute of Maritime Studies, Nantucket, Mass.

FIGURE 4: The Captain and Betsey Baxter's House, Built ca. 1682, 10 Broadway. *The nineteenth-century inhabitants of 'Sconset creatively named their homes to evoke the peaceful atmosphere and history of the village. The Baxters named their home "Saint's Rest" and also kept a quarterboard from the 1852 wreck of the ship* Shanunga *that hung on the property. The present owners of the home have named their small guest cottage Saint's Rest and kept the name* Shanunga *for the main house.*

children who lived in town began to join the men for long stays in the spring and fall during their fishing seasons. As a result, the primitive shelters were improved. Dirt or clay floors were covered with wood, interior walls were finished with plaster, exteriors were given a layer of shingles over simple sheathing, and brick chimneys were installed.[10] Edward F. Underhill (1830–1898), a New York State court stenographer by profession and a businessman by inclination, was a history buff and an ardent admirer of 'Sconset's whale houses. He wrote of the exterior and interior improvements made after 1800: "old clinker-built [tightly spaced clapboards] roofs were taken off, and replaced side by side and covered with shingles, to discourage the rain from trying to become too familiar with the interiors."[11] Underhill also reported: "A startling in[n]ovation was made by a well-to-do fisherman that aroused the jealous criticism of all his neighbors. He actually caused the interior of his dwelling to be plastered! For years he was the subject of animadversion, and it did not cease until the last family was able to indulge in the same extravagance."[12]

Said to have been one of those moved from Sesachacha to 'Sconset, the "Shanunga" at 10 Broadway, built circa 1682, is one of the oldest examples of a whale house[13] (FIGURE 4). Like many of the 'Sconset cottages, it also has an interesting social history. A nine-teenth-century owner, Betsey Cary (1778–1860), used the cottage as a tav-ern, having a tap room of eight by ten feet. The home was inherited by Cary's daughter, Betsey (1806–1883), who married the former whaleman Captain William Baxter (1805–?). A well-known character around the vil-lage, Baxter converted the cottage/tavern into a cottage/post office and appointed himself the postmaster of 'Sconset. According to local tradi-tion, when Captain Baxter "came over the hill on Main Street [into the vil-lage], he tooted his fish horn, and the event of the day was the gathering of the people at the [post office] window, and for each letter or paper received, one whole cent went into the coffers of the rasping old mariner! And yet there are those who boldly assert that he did not get rich!"[14] The present owner of the Shanunga suggests that a thin, worn slot cut in the door on the southeast side of the house was once the official outgoing postal box.[15]

Spanning several centuries, the evolution of construction of the Shanunga remains discernable from its east-facing facade. The first phase of the seventeenth-century structure is the south portion, originally a sin-gle room of twelve by fifteen feet. The room was open to the peak and had a spare interior. Sleeping quarters were arranged by a partition several feet from the south gable wall, which was further divided at the top into a sleeping garret—known from its fifteenth-century Welsh origin as a "hanging-loft."[16] Particular to the Shanunga, the central living space had also been partitioned into a sleeping loft above the entire room. The simple rectangular great room (for cooking, dining, and living) and the hanging-loft was the first of several phases in the evolution of the plan of the Shanunga and most whale houses (FIGURE 5).

After 1700, additional space was integrated into the whale house through the addition of low sheds projecting from the sleeping quarters on both the east and west side of the first floor. These two small lean-to expansions or "warts" push outward from the structure's core room, cre-ating a T-shape plan. The distinct combination of the first-phase and sec-ond-phase extensions defines the unmistakable "double lean-to form" of the 'Sconset whale house.

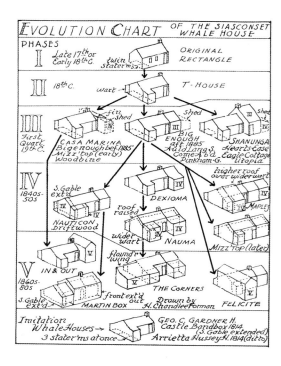

FIGURE 5: Henry C. Forman, Evolution Chart of the Siasconset Whale Houses, ca. 1966. Pen and ink drawing. *Published in H.C. Forman,* Early Nantucket and Its Whale Houses *(Nantucket, Mass.: Mill Hill Press, reprint 1991), 130.*

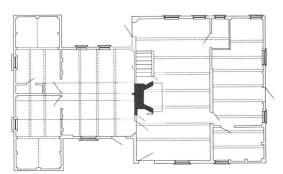

{ LEFT }
FIGURE 6: Plan of
Shanunga. Illustration by
Richard Valdes, 2003. *This
drawing shows the evolution
of the plan of the house, as
it was built between 1682
and 1800.*

{ RIGHT }
FIGURE 7: Shanunga
Interior. *Wood-paneled
walls in the cottage
Shanunga date to the mid-
nineteenth century.*

None of the early T-shape houses are intact, however, as all were further extended and recon-figured in several directions both outward and, in some cases, upward. The Shanunga for instance has a large one-and-a-half-story section on its north side, opposite the early T-shape group of rooms. Built circa 1760–80, the addition accommodated a kitchen without obliterating the earliest portions of the dwelling (FIGURE 6). With this new kitchen came a chimney with a hearth located on the north side of the room. Yet another extension to the kitchen on its north side was added circa 1800, at which time the hearth was moved to the south wall and walls were improved. Modernization was desirable into the twentieth century, but the early nineteenth-century fireplace and its antique character remain (FIGURE 7).

Practical and utilitarian improvements, plus the installation of dormers, porches, and exten-sions (warts and all), having more to do with personal taste and whimsy, occurred throughout the centuries on the cottages and continue in guided moderation today.[17] After speaking with the octoge-narians living in the whale houses, Edward Underhill reported that: "the visitor who knew Siasconset previous to 1880, would be surprised to note changes in the appearance of many of the old cottages. . . . [They] have been increased in their proportions by putting a story on the 'warts,' or by projections covered with shingles laid on in shapes fantastic enough to satisfy the longings of the most ardent admirer of incongrous [sic] house building."[18]

Copyright 1905 by the Rotograph Co.
A 7006   "Auld Lang Syne" (oldest house) Siasconset, Mass

Despite these expansions necessary for modern life, the overall intimate scale of the whale houses has survived. Once strictly practical, these former fishermen's cottages grew to be valued for both their simplicity of design and petite charms (FIGURE 8). As R. B. Hussey stated in his travel guide of 1889: "[L]ife at Sconset is emphatically a cottage life. The old village is made up of fisherman's ancient huts transmogrified into pleasing villas of modern pretentions, rendering the combination of architecture both quaint and unique, and the cottages both doll-like and commodious."[19]

A perennial favorite, recorded in countless postcards, paintings, and photographs, "Auld Lang Syne," built circa 1675, at 6 Broadway, is thought to be the oldest house on the island (FIGURE 9).[20] Its plan has the essential character of a whale house and includes a hanging loft that is accessed with a ladder. The ladder remains despite several alterations that were installed gradually over its three-hundred-year history. Following the typical early construction evolution, Auld Lang Syne grew from one room to a T-shape plan. After 1790 a kitchen was added,[21] and a small wart sprouted on the west side sometime after 1890. Within the last several years, the house was again refurbished: walls were improved and insulated, new windows installed, the house reshingled, the northwest shed roof was lowered, and some interior walls reconfigured. Even though the exterior fabric of the

{ OPPOSITE }

FIGURE 8: Auld Lang Syne, Built in 1675, at 6 Broadway. *As this photograph indicates, the climate and soil of Siasconset are particularly suited to growing roses, hydrangeas, and hollyhocks in great abundance.*

{ ABOVE }

FIGURE 9: Auld Lang Syne, 1905. *This turn-of-the-century view helps envision the small scale of this old whale cottage, built for Captain Henry Coleman.* Courtesy of the Nantucket Historical Association.

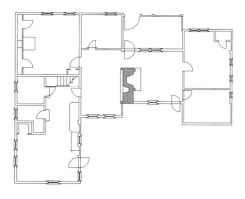

cottage was not significantly disturbed, some neighbors raised objections and questioned the extent of the renovation.[22]

Built circa 1806–09 or prior,[23] "Hearts Ease," at 14 Center Street also evolved in the typical eighteenth-century fashion. Over time, it was greatly expanded to the north (FIGURE 10). Depicted in a twentieth-century artist's rendering, the whale house plan is still recognizable (FIGURE 11). Apart from the easy to distinguish former whale houses, many others have been altered and layered over the years to the point where the basic T-shape design is no longer apparent. Cottages such as Casa Marina or Sans Souci have interesting warts, porches, raised roofs, and various punctures. The whale houses also have delightful nautical or quixotic historic elements such as portholes, unmatched windows, miniature doors, and construction materials salvaged from shipwrecks that give the neighborhood a "patchwork" appearance. For the most part, it is obvious that present-day homeowners do not wish to alter the small scale of the cottages. As Forman wrote of Hearts Ease, "This is the honeymooner's dream of a snuggery...."[24] Tightly fitted along 'Sconset's historic lanes of Front Street, Broadway, Center, and Shell streets,[25] the delightful group of whale cottages form the heart of one of the most unique and picturesque villages in New England (FIGURE 12).

A visitor to Nantucket in 1772, J. Hector St. John de Crèvecoeur wrote the following description of 'Sconset: "I have never seen a spot better calculated to cherish contemplative ideas; perfectly unconnected with the great world, and far removed from its perturbations."[26] Long acknowledged for its quietude and simplicity of lifestyle, 'Sconset's appeal as a rural vacation spot was recognized in the 1830s by residents from the town of Nantucket. Many of the fishing shanties and former whale

{ LEFT }
FIGURE 10: Plan of Hearts Ease. Illustration by Richard Valdes, 2003. *In this drawing, sections of this house, dating from circa 1809 to the late twentieth century, are shown from right to left respectively.*

{ RIGHT }
FIGURE 11: Jane Brewster Reid (1862–1966), Heart's Ease, ca. 1935. Watercolor on paper. *Picturesque cottages of 'Sconset have been popular subject matter for generations of artists. This cottage was built at 14 Center Street around 1806.* Courtesy of the Nantucket Historical Association. Gift of Mr. and Mrs. Max Berry, 86.46.4.

FIGURE 12: View of
Broadway, 'Sconset, at the
Turn of the Twentieth
Century. *Not just one or
two examples of the whale
houses survive, but rather an
entire community of early
vernacular architecture.*
Courtesy of the Nantucket
Historical Association.

houses were rented during the summer months to Nantucketers seeking a peaceful retreat from the bustle of urban life. In addition to the renters, Nantucket's wealthy whaling merchants and seafaring families built their own vacation cottages. In a journal entry dated 1842, Obed Macy wrote: "The fishing business still continues to be kept up with many that make it their dependanse [sic], in the Fall and Spring. But the greater part of the people that go to Siasconset, go out for their health, and others for the sake of the ride, and in parties of pleasure.... How different is this, than it was 50 or 60 years ago,—when very few visited Siasconset except it was for business or profit."[27]

Matthew Crosby (1791–1878)—son-in-law of one of Nantucket's wealthiest whaling merchants, Zenas Coffin (1764–1828), and a successful businessman himself—contracted with Charles Pendleton "to build him a House at Siasconsitt [sic] to be completed on or before the first day of May 1837." According to Pendleton's contract with Crosby, the house was to be thirty-three feet wide by twenty feet deep and "set up on pillars 2 ½ ft high in front[.] Terrace five ft wide with Balestrade all round."[28] Crosby was, perhaps, requesting a porch for his vacation house. Captain Seth Pinkham (1786–1844) and his family who lived in a typical Nantucket house on Fair Street in town, found 'Sconset to be an enjoyable retreat as well. A descendant of Pinkham, Florence Anderson wrote in her memoir of the family: "[Pinkham] was among the *elite* in owning a house at Siasconset. This he had purchased of Father Brown, a very old building, of queer angles of roof and yet queerer irregularities in window arrangement."[29] Although the particular cottage to which Anderson is referring is

{ ABOVE LEFT }
FIGURE 13: Unknown Artist, Eunice Starbuck Hadwen, ca. 1820. Oil on panel. Courtesy of the Nantucket Historical Association. Gift of Eunice Barney Swain, 1915. 15.23.1

{ ABOVE RIGHT }
FIGURE 14: 20 Main Street, 'Sconset, Built in 1837. *This neatly appointed single-story cottage was one of the first cottages built by a resident of Nantucket Town as a summer home in 'Sconset. As most of its buildings date to the mid-nineteenth century, 'Sconset is considered one of the earliest resorts in New England*

{ BELOW }
FIGURE 16: Bird's Eye View of 'Sconset, Detail from "Bird's Eye View of the Town of Nantucket," 1881. Lithograph, published by J. J. Stoner, printed by Beck & Pauli, Madison, Wisconsin. Courtesy of the Nantucket Historical Association.

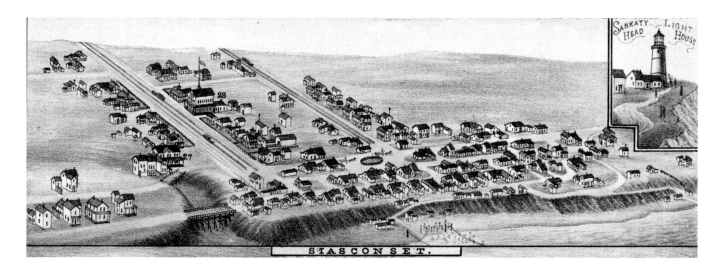

FIGURE 15: Greetings From 'Sconset. *Pictured in this old postcard are a group of fishing shanties turned vacation cottages.* Courtesy of the Nantucket Historical Association.

FIGURE 17:
Edward Fitch Underhill,
Engraving ca. Mid- to
Late Nineteenth Century.
Print Collection, Miriam and Ira
D. Wallach, Division of Art,
Prints and Photographs, The New
York Public Library, Astor,
Lenox, and Tilden Foundations.

not known, it may be that the "queer" building was a converted fisherman's house. Certainly numbered among the elite, Eunice Hadwen (1799–1864, FIGURE 13), the wife of one of Nantucket's most prosperous whaling merchants, William Hadwen (1791–1862), also had a vacation home in 'Sconset, located at 20 Main Street. The home was first built circa 1837 for Frederick W. Mitchell and sold to Eunice Hadwen in 1855.[30] The one-story house with its simple colonnade porch also had twin gable chimneys (FIGURE 14). It was initially, as would be expected for rural 'Sconset, a less elaborate and smaller version of the refined Federal-style homes that graced Nantucket Town.

When the whale fishery that provided great wealth to so many ceased to be, the whole of Nantucket was plunged into severe economic depression, and Nantucket Town and 'Sconset village lost a significant portion of their populations. Over a period of twenty-five years, houses fell into disrepair or were dismantled and removed to the mainland. However, a second wave of settlement came to the island in the last quarter of the nineteenth century. These inhabitants, like the Wampanoag and initial colonists, were interested in the offerings of the sea—as a base for pleasure rather than toil. The sweet air and mild climate of 'Sconset lured people from the mainland who sought a peaceful seaside vacation (FIGURE 15). By 1877, an article in the *Inquirer and Mirror* described the island's summer visitors as a "throng" with "hotels in 'waiting orders' for the many others who will be compelled to seek refuge on the seaboard from the heat and vapid atmosphere of cities."[31] The newspaper also noted: "The aspect of the ancient and unique village of Siasconset, distant a pleasant drive from town, is modernized and rendered quite attractive by the tiny *cottages ornee* which have lately been erected. From the piazzas of these there is a fine inland view of the surrounding landscape, and also an outlook upon the illimitable ocean, unsurpassed, if not unequalled, from any point along the Atlantic coast, with nothing to interrupt the view save snow-white sails swelling with every breeze—ships and vessels" (FIGURE 16).[32]

In the late nineteenth century, Edward Underhill (FIGURE 17) wrote specifically on the history and charms of the whale houses to promote the village as a vacation destination. Booklets by Underhill and his wife,

{ OPPOSITE }

FIGURE 18: Cap'n's Gig, At 1 Lily Street, Built ca. 1889. *The "Underhill cottages" located on Evelyn, Lily, and Pochick streets were especially popular with the actors' colony. Famed actor and comedian Robert Benchley once summered at the cottage pictured here.*

{ ABOVE }

FIGURE 19: Bo'sn's Bunt, Built ca. 1889, 2 Lily Street. *This cottage is among the smallest in the Underhill neighborhood. "If an extra room was needed, Mr. Underhill had that figured out too. He built a separate room on wheels which hauled by a large mule, could be attached for the summer to whichever house required it."* Quoted from Margaret Fawcett Barnes, *'Sconset Heyday* (Nantucket, Mass.: The Island Press, 1969).

Evelyn, include *'Sconset by the Sea,*[33] *The Old Houses on 'Sconset Bank,*[34] *'Sconset in a Nutshell,*[35] *A Pictyure Booke of ye Pachworke Vyllage Sconsett by ye Sea Ye Pictyures was drawn from others made by Master Wyere and Master Platte by ye Helpe of ye Sunn,*[36] and *The Credible Chronicles of the Patchwork Village.*[37] Recognizing the quiet, simple beauty of the old dwellings, Underhill emulated their design in a development of equally small-size cottages located southwest of the neighborhood of the whale houses. Built by local Nantucket carpenters, the Underhill cottages form their own enclave on Lily Street, Evelyn Street (named for his daughter and wife), and Everett, Magnolia, and Pochick streets. The Cap'n's Gig at 1 Lily Street and the Bo'sn's Bunt at 2 Lily Street (both built circa 1889) are examples of only two of the several variations (FIGURES 18, 19). In constructing the houses, Underhill incorporated a variety of low, shed-roof warts in order to model his cottages on the seemingly random two-hundred-year evolution of the older houses.

As seen at the Observatory cottage (FIGURE 20), built circa 1888–89 at 6 Lily Street, Underhill employed a one-story, double-lean-to plan recognizable from the third phase of the whale houses. Opposite the double-lean-to is a one-and-a-half-story gabled room with a one-story wedge-shaped form projecting in front of it.

Apparent in the interior at the Observatory is the effort to arrange the rooms in the traditional way, with bedrooms partitioned off the central living area. The open rafters and walls, as well as the overall small size, contribute to the informal nature of the structure (FIGURE 21). The casual order and diminutive qualities of the cottage were certainly meant to captivate visitors. From the *Nantucket Journal* of August 4, 1887, "Old Seaweeds" wrote: "The capacity of a 'Sconset cottage is phenomenal. There are so many who partake of their daily bread in one on Evelyn Street, that in order to eat all at once it is said they have to sit spoon fashion around the table. At another on Lily Street, sofas and cots are brought into nightly requisition for the adults, the children are hung on pegs around the rooms. Captain William Baxter is the authority for this last statement. He says he knows it is true because he has seen one of the pegs."[38]

FIGURE 20: The Observatory, Built ca. 1888–89, 6 Lily Street. *The one-story shed roof front projection, which can be seen in this cottage, is said to be called a "flounder." The wedged-shaped form was adapted by Edward Underhill from additions found on the whale houses, specifically in the cottage known as "The Corners," located near the former 'Sconset water pump.*

FIGURE 21: Interior of the Observatory. *A thought on cottage accommodations from one of Edward Underhill's many newspaper ads: "Rents $90 and $175 for the season. N.B.: I provide cribs and cradles. There my responsibility ends. Tenants must furnish babies for themselves."*

Due to his aggressive and often humorous marketing strategies, including the booklets, newspaper ads, romanticized histories, storytelling narratives, and health testimonials by doctors, the rental of Underhill's miniature vacation houses was wildly popular. The *Nantucket Journal* reported, "Mr. E. F. Underhill has rented all of his cottages, and is daily turning cottage seekers away. He could rent a dozen more if he had them."[39] An advertisement of June 1898 in the *Inquirer and Mirror* listed: "At Siasconset, 85 cottages completely furnished. Rent from $75 to $175 for the season." A few weeks after the ad was placed, Edward Underhill died suddenly in New York. His obituary states that Underhill was "highly esteemed" and that "largely through his unique efforts the little hamlet has attained a widespread notoriety, and no opportunity was ever lost by the deceased to urge its attractions as a place of summer resort."[40]

Underhill was not the first to see the potential of advertising 'Sconset's mild seaside weather and history to off-islanders. In addition to Underhill, two of 'Sconset's earliest off-island builder/developers were Charles H. Robinson and Franklin Ellis, who established the Sunset Heights neighborhood in 1873, across a gully south of the ancient whale houses.[41] Robinson's fondness for Victorian styles of architecture led the way for both individuals and developers to follow. Houses erected in the Gothic Revival, high Victorian, Stick, and Shingle styles, forming an arc around the nucleus of ancient whale cottages, expanded the borders of the village. The exalted level of massing and ornamentation of these romantic styles reflected the taste of the period. There were numerous sizeable Victorian houses built along the oceanfront bluff, as well as smaller homes and cottages built throughout the village. Mixed in with the grand vacation houses (FIGURES 26, 27), less formal architecture was also a choice for the casual lifestyle of the resort area and the small scale of 'Sconset. A high Victorian Gothic design such as 'Sconset's Union Chapel, built in 1882 for the multi-denominational vacationers, was a moderate interpretation of the style when originally built.[42] Twentieth-century decorative subtractions and reconfigurations have further muted the chapel's architectural flourishes (FIGURE 22). Although many houses and buildings were modified in the twentieth century, Victorian architectural features and massing are still

{ OPPOSITE }

FIGURE 22: Union Chapel, Built in 1882. *Servicing visitors of varied religious persuasions, the chapel was originally constructed in a high Victorian style that was later simplified. Characteristic features of the Victorian era are still visible in the pointed arch windows and Gothic-style "flying buttresses," appropriately clad in shingles.*

{ OPPOSITE }
FIGURE 23: The Flaggship, Built in 1890, 12 Baxter Road.
The glass enclosure on the porch is a late twentieth-century addition. It is a most necessary feature on the windy bluff where the cottage is located.

{ ABOVE }
FIGURE 24: Detail of the Flaggship's Mansard Roof.

plainly visible on houses in all sections of the village. The North Bluff, an area that has its start at the edge of the old fishing cottages and continues north to Sankaty Head Lighthouse, was purchased and developed over the course of several years by William J. Flagg (1818–1898), an Ohio- and New York–based businessman and writer. Flagg inspired a new era of home building in his Sankaty Heights development when he had a summer home constructed just south of the lighthouse.[43] A story is told of one Asa Jones, a fisherman and former Nantucket carpenter, who was forced to stow his hammer and saws for twenty-five years as the islanders suffered through an economic depression. When Flagg asked Jones to build a house for him, the carpenter, in great disbelief, asked Flagg to repeat the offer. He did and Jones constructed a house circa 1875, igniting the construction of new vacation homes.[44]

Further north along Baxter Road is the second house Flagg had built as a summer home. The nine-hundred-square-foot cottage, called the Flaggship, was built in 1890[45] in the Second Empire style (FIGURE 23). It appears that Flagg, a wealthy man who could well afford a large, ornate house, chose to be fashionable yet modest, by considerably toning down this most ebullient, French-inspired Victorian fashion. The Flaggship has the definite hallmarks of the style: a mansard roof and roof dormers, tall windows, and a projecting second story over an eastward-facing porch. In place of the bold articulation, curving forms and three-dimensionality found on most Second Empire designs, this house has a flat-sided and slightly pitched mansard roof, unbracketed shallow eaves, pedimented but simple roof dormers, a single square mass, and an exterior sheathed in shingles (painted clapboards were the usual choice). An interesting detail, the shingles on several rows of the roof and the dormer pediments are cut in a scallop pattern, echoing the slate roofing tiles that were favored for this style (FIGURE 24).

Over the decades, as practical needs and tastes changed, the Flaggship did have a single-room expansion and alterations. However, during a restoration of the house in 1998 by 'Sconset residents and preservation architects Elizabeth Churchill and David Bentley, this husband-and-wife team were given the opportunity to remove twentieth-century

additions and return the building to its essential original configuration.[46] Keeping a house small in today's real estate market, especially on prestigious Baxter Road, is not usual. Churchill and Bentley are most concerned about the tremendous temptation many architects, builders, and homeowners have to tear down and rebuild larger to fill the broad lots along the bluff. The conundrum of preservation verses modernization of the island's historic architecture has been under way at least since the 1880s, when Underhill lamented the changes he saw occurring in the ancient whale houses. Henry Forman, who spent years examining the whale houses inside and out, was also alarmed by what he termed, the "successive uglifications" of the cottages. In his book, Forman called for "a historic zoning law rigidly enforced down to the smallest details."[47] Presently, Nantucket's Historic District Commission strives to protect the houses and regulate renovation, but the elected committee cannot monitor every detail. Some homeowners choose to gut interiors completely, while others believe that the historic homes are not worth saving at all.[48]

An example of both thoughtful restoration and modernization is 12 Baxter Road. Built sometime between 1885 and 1894,[49] this home underwent several additions and changes over a period of many decades (FIGURE 25).[50] First erected during the last phase of the Victorian era, the two-and-a-half-story, organically massed house is a blend of styles—a common occurrence in the vernacular architecture of the village. Archival photographs of the late nineteenth century show the house with a steep-pitch gable end to the south, a gabled roof dormer over an elongated window, and a small porch below, the features of early Victorian designs. The pointed dormer remains, but the small porch was removed and the south gable almost completely obscured by a stocky, conical-roof two-story bay extension, added circa 1904–09. This two-story projecting bay with ribbon windows (multipaned casements) are characteristic of the popular, late-nineteenth-century Shingle style (SEE ALSO FIGURES 26 AND 27).[51] Additional Shingle-style characteristics of 12 Baxter Road include low-sloping shed dormers, an organic plan, and a complete exterior covering of shingles. These early-twentieth-century alterations may have reflected changing taste and a move away from earlier Victorian styles. The current

{ OPPOSITE }

FIGURE 25: 12 Baxter Road, Built ca. 1885–94. *A second-story porch wraps around the north section of this house and is accessed from the living room. Wide porches are a typical feature of late-nineteenth-century cottages in 'Sconset.*

{ OPPOSITE }

FIGURE 26: 23 Morey Lane, Built ca. 1904. *This eastward-facing house with leaded diamond-paned windows, continuous shingle cladding, and widely encompassing roof line is an outstanding example of the Shingle style. With its roots in colonial architecture (plentiful on Nantucket), the design recalled the simplicity of sturdy, timber-frame houses. Unpainted, shingle-clad, organically designed homes like 23 Morey Lane were especially popular in 'Sconset at the turn of the nineteenth century. The shingled balconies are a recent addition, but perfectly integrated into the character of the house.*

{ ABOVE }

FIGURE 27: Interior of 23 Morey Lane. *A dramatic brick fireplace recalls the massiveness of colonial-era fireplaces. Once the vacation home of silent film actor and 'Sconset regular Robert Hilliard, the giant hearth would have been an appropriate backdrop for an actor who is said to have had a valet with him to hold his brocaded dressing gown while he went for a swim.*

homeowner also had a need for a few alterations. A modern kitchen was added, and, at a later date, the homeowner returned to Nantucket's Historic District Commission for the approval of a small shed dormer on the third-floor roof. The committee requested that the application for the dormer be withdrawn as it did not fit with the historic structure.[52] After being presented with evidence of its previous existence, noted in late-nineteenth-century photographs of the house, the Historic District Commission did eventually approve the request.

Extensions to an original structure, occurring over the course of many decades, are not an uncommon sight in cottages and houses of 'Sconset and Nantucket Town. Rear additions may not always be seen from the front of the house (Introduction, FIGURE 4, Mill Street), and lateral expansions can also be unobtrusive. Added rooms allow for modernization and are often accomplished without disrupting the historic fabric of the original building. Such is the case at 12 Baxter Road and 20 Main Street in 'Sconset (FIGURE 14). In the latter, the original section of the house was built well before the Victorian era.[53] Presently known as Green Chimneys (named recently for the many stacks that dot the roof), the 20 Main Street house has a contiguous arrangement of an abundance of rooms. The original north-facing home was preserved but greatly extended on the southeast section. Prior to the 1920s, a detached, arched-entrance horse stall was located at the rear of the dwelling. After 1923, the arch-way design of the stall became inspiration for a porch. Numerous additions and small structures continued to be incorporated over the years up to the present, resulting in its meandering, railroad-car-like connection of rooms (FIGURE 28).[54] The long group of rooms wraps around and back nearly to the front of the house, leaving a center yard that is almost completely hidden from view (FIGURE 29).

Green Chimneys has been renovated for comfort and carefully preserved to maintain respect for its historic value, as have a similar group of structures located south across a gully just off Ocean Avenue. The little houses at 4 Cottage Avenue (FIGURE 30) have been reconfigured since their original construction sometime between 1873 and 1898.[55] During their 130-year history the cottages were sited adjacent to (and may have

{ ABOVE }

FIGURE 28: Interior of 20 Main Street, 'Sconset, ca. early 1900s. Courtesy of the Nantucket Historical Association.

{ OPPOSITE }

FIGURE 29: Green Chimneys. *Many additions to this one-story cottage look as though they have grown naturally around a center yard. Painted shingles and trim effectively unify the many sections of the whole.*

{ OPPOSITE }

FIGURE 30: 4 Cottage Avenue, Built Between 1873 and 1898. *Once part of the Moby Dick Inn, this set of cottages is now privately owned. To join the separate rooms openings were created in adjoining walls and two baths were combined to make a kitchen.*

{ ABOVE }

FIGURE 31: Interior of 4 Cottage Avenue. *The exposed-rafter construction, low-gable roof, and general small scale of this cottage is reminiscent of seventeenth-century whale houses in 'Sconset.*

originally been part of) an inn called the 'Sconset Cottage Club, circa 1910–12.[56] The central building of the Cottage Club was later known under several names, including the Old 'Sconset Inn, the Moby Dick, and at present, the Summer House.

Built in stages, with additions and reconfigurations occurring sporadically from the 1920s through the 1940s,[57] 4 Cottage Avenue is another one-story rambling arrangement of connected rooms wrapped around a center yard. The single structure, composed of six separate private rental cottages, each with a tiny bath (FIGURE 31), was purchased by the present homeowner, actor John Shea, in 1979, when the cottages were a part of the Moby Dick. Shortly after being purchased, the private rooms were transformed into one house and a detached master bedroom cottage was built to create a buffer between the home and the Moby Dick.[58] Both the interior and exterior of the new cottage look as though they were part of the original set of rooms.

Preservation of the cottage tradition was a purposeful decision made by Shea for several reasons. In the early 1970s while he was in drama school, before his own acting career was established, he waited tables and provided room service to several theater and film personalities summering at the Moby Dick, including J. Gibbs "Gibby" Penrose and James Cagney. In purchasing the former rental cottages and while restoring them, Shea and his wife, artist Melissa MacLeod,[59] were consciously making an effort to preserve the historic integrity of the structures, as well as carry on the vacation tradition of the actors' colony and artistic retreat. Echoing both the ancient whale houses and the Underhill cottages in design and spirit, the little conglomeration at 4 Cottage Avenue perfectly illustrates the thoughtful renovation, respect for the historic record, and the charm and pleasure found in 'Sconset's vernacular architecture.

'Sconset Actors' Colony

AIMEE E. NEWELL

New York Actresses Mary Shaw and Nanette Comstock in Siasconset with Friends, ca. 1905. *Shaw, who managed theatrical productions at the 'Sconset Casino, and Comstock enjoy a game of medicine ball in front of Nippintucket, an Underhill cottage on Pochick Street.* Courtesy of the Nantucket Historical Association.

IN THE EARLY TWENTIETH CENTURY, New York City's famed Great White Way stretched all the way to the village of Siasconset on the eastern shores of Nantucket Island. "Delightful 'Sconset," as it was affectionately known, even had its own Broadway, one block from the bank. New York's Broadway actors first discovered 'Sconset's Broadway in the 1890s, and soon put the village on the map as an actors' colony.

In the decades before central air-conditioning, New York City heat proved oppressive for actors and audiences alike, forcing Broadway theaters to be dark during the summer months. To seek relief and relaxation New York actors journeyed to 'Sconset, attracted by the village's cool ocean breezes, saltwater bathing, picturesque architecture, and quiet life. In 1893, the *New York Dramatic Mirror* published a letter from the actress May Robson singing the praises of the village. "Do you know anything about the quaint little Nantucket village of Siasconset?" she wrote. "If not, steal a week from sizzling New York and come here, to sea breezes and moonlight nights. Somehow, actors and actresses always find out these heavenly spots to make delightful idiots of themselves in, don't they?"

Among the first actors to discover 'Sconset, in the mid- to late 1890s, were famed stage stars George Fawcett and his wife, Percy Haswell. They eventually bought a house on 'Sconset's Main Street and named it "Rosemary," after a play that Haswell was performing at the time. Another actor, Harry Woodruff, had an "upside-down" house built on Morey Lane, with four bedrooms on the lower floor and one spacious room on the second floor, maximizing the spectacular views.

The Underhill cottages, located on Evelyn, Lily, and Pochick streets, were especially popular with the actors' colony. Margaret Fawcett Barnes recalled that these cottages seem to have had "a hundred years of sporadic living in them . . . you rambled through rooms, some with such low ceilings you might be on a ship; you mounted stairs so steep they must have been patterned from a ship's companionway."

By 1910 there were almost five hundred actors and theatrical people summering in 'Sconset, including such well-known personalities as Mary Shaw, Robert Hilliard, Joseph Jefferson, Lillian Russell, and gossip columnist Hedda Hopper. Although as Barnes explained, 'Sconset offered "relief to play-folk who had spent most of their winter months in and out of costumes and in the public gaze," these same actors could not resist the opportunity to perform for the community. Completed in 1900, the Siasconset Casino held its first production in August of that year, for a full house of 820 people. The evening included a wide variety of acts—plays, songs, dances, and recitals—performed by 'Sconset's famed summer residents.

As the actors knew all too well, all shows must come to a close, and 'Sconset's run as an actors' colony came to an end in the 1920s. Moving pictures offered Broadway actors year-round employment in California, and New York theaters installed air-conditioning, allowing them to stay open in the summer. But, as Margaret Fawcett Barnes pointed out, "the gaiety and the glamour of the Stage rubbed off on the ['Sconset] life and left it a little more gleaming."

{ CHAPTER *6* }

Bungalows:
Cozy Havens and Summer Retreats

Margaret Moore Booker

*T*HE most stylish thing in architecture, at present, is the Bungle-oh, and the Bungled Life is the life to lead. In the summer, at least, every self-respecting soul leaves his 'appy 'ome, builds, begs, borrows, or rents a Bungle-oh, and settles down in some mosquito-haunted spot," wrote a journalist in 1912 for *Country Life in America* magazine.[1]

Although the writer was being tongue-in-cheek, he accurately conveys the popularity of the bungalow as a vacation cottage. The small size, simple and informal design, and inexpensive building costs made the bungalow an attractive style for vacationers, and bungalows began appearing on Nantucket in the early 1900s. By this date many middle-class families could afford to own a second home,[2] and Nantucket, known as the "Bermuda of the north Atlantic,"[3] was the perfect location, drawing increasing crowds in the summer. As one 1908 design book states, bungalows were perfect holiday homes because they had "restfulness of appearance [that] refreshes the tired city dweller" and were "homey...that ideal you have seen in the dreamy shadows of night when...you have yearned for a haven of rest."[4] Bungalows—a distinctly American house type—were built on Nantucket through the 1940s, eventually as year-round residences, not just seasonal retreats.[5]

At one point there were more than 120 bungalows on Nantucket, and examples of the style can be found in most neighborhoods on the island today, including 'Sconset.[6] As compared to the complex and eclectic Victorian designs of the late nineteenth century, these bungalows represent a sparse and rustic aesthetic evocative of simple living and tranquil retreats. As Arts and Crafts movement leader Gustav Stickley explained in 1903, the American bungalow is "a summer residence of extreme simplicity, of economic construction and intended for more or less primitive living."[7] Much like the earlier styles of architecture built on the island, the bungalow was adapted to the Nantucket aesthetic by local builders.

The bungalow style, with its practical floor plan, built-in features, and good ventilation, appealed to Nantucket homeowners and vacationers who were intrigued by the prospect of modern living. In

{ OPPOSITE }

FIGURE 1: 47 West Chester Street, Built in 1915. *"The simplest kind of stucco house can be made a dwelling of personality and charm through a careful use of color....It is suggested that the walls be of white rough troweled stucco with roofs of variegated red tile."* (Small Homes of Architectural Distinction, *Harper & Brothers, 1929).*

161

the first decades of the twentieth century, conveniences such as wireless telegraphy, electricity, long-distance telephone lines, the automobile, and the airplane were introduced or expanded on Nantucket and slowly began to challenge the quiet and quaint qualities of island life. In one effort to protect the island's old-fashioned charm, Nantucketers successfully banned automobiles until 1918.

By the early 1900s the island's year-round population had dwindled to less than three thousand and the summertime population climbed to twelve thousand. The bungalow was one form of building that met the increased demand for rental properties. Advertisements for bungalows for sale or available to rent appeared frequently in the Nantucket *Inquirer and Mirror* in the 1910s and 1920s, indicating just how popular this style of home was on the island. Builders and realtors promoted lots that were "suitable for bungalows," and notices of bungalows being built were common. For instance, in March 1917 it was reported that "Ralph Pierce is building a bachelor's bungalow below the bank,"[8] and in October 1915, "Reginald Hussey is building an attractive little bungalow on the southern shore of Broad Creek."[9] This was part of a general building boom on the island in the first two decades of the century, as the following report from the *Inquirer and Mirror* of March 1915 suggests: "If you take a drive [in a horse-drawn carriage] about town at the present time, what will strike you more forcibly than anything else will probably be the large amount of building in progress, and especially the number of new houses in process of construction or remodeling."[10]

The most interesting example of the Craftsman-style bungalow on Nantucket was built in 1915 (FIGURE 1) on land owned by Oscar Edward Quigley (1893–1967) on West Chester Street, at the corner of New Lane. A Canadian-born mason, contractor, and architect, Quigley[11] probably designed and built the house on spec, as he quickly turned it over that same

{ TOP }

FIGURE 2: Gable Peaks, 47 West Chester. *The oriental influence of the bungalow style is evident in this bungalow's upswept gable peaks and dormer windows.*

{ BOTTOM }

FIGURE 3: Dormer Window, 47 West Chester.

year to John S. Grouard (1867–1927), a highly respected physician and surgeon on the island.[12] One of the most visually striking features of the bungalow is the bright white stucco facade, on wood frame construction—it is one of only a handful of stucco buildings on the island.[13] Island carpenter and builder Arthur A. Norcross (1868–1944)[14] framed the building, and it is likely that Quigley did the finishing stucco work himself. The relatively sparse facade with dark green trim, dramatic overhanging eaves, and a red shingle roof give this Craftsman-style bungalow a stark modern feeling that is a startling departure from the historic gray-shingled saltbox and lean-to structures that dominate the neighborhood.[15]

An unusual feature of 47 West Chester is the strong oriental influence present in the building: the upswept gable peaks (FIGURE 2) and elaborate dormer windows (FIGURE 3) are reminiscent of Japanese pagodas. Also rare for Nantucket are the massive porch columns that resemble Prairie Style houses, developed by Frank Lloyd Wright and other Chicago architects around 1900 to 1920.[16]

The oriental influence and use of stucco—a durable finish generally composed of cement, sand, and lime that gives a textured, handcrafted appearance—are frequently seen in Craftsman bungalows, a style of building that was predominant in America from 1890 to 1940. The West Chester Street home has many of the typical characteristics of this style, including low dimensions, gently pitched broad gables, wide window openings, ridge beams that extend beyond the wall and roofline, a gabled dormer window, and a front porch tucked beneath a gable. The oriental and Craftsman style details in 47 West Chester are reminiscent of the work of architects Charles Sumner Greene and Henry Mather Greene, known simply as Greene and Greene, who are well known for their Craftsman-style bungalows built in California in the early 1900s.[17] During their formative years as architecture students, in the late 1880s and early 1890s, the brothers actually spent their summers on Nantucket and made many drawings of the island landscape and buildings, which clearly appealed to their artistic sensibilities.[18]

Nantucket bungalows generally have wood shingle or clapboard facades, and most have a prominent front porch. One of the virtues of a bungalow is its intimate relationship with nature, and porches were seen as a way to unify indoor and outdoor life. Examples of the style on island vary from modest, single-story homes with low-pitched roofs, such as 25 York Street and 20 Milk Street, to more elaborate, rustically detailed types like the single-story home called The Last Resort (FIGURE 4). Located on Hinckley Lane (named for Eben Hinckley, who had a farm in the area), the latter is a particularly interesting Craftsman-style bungalow with broad overhanging eaves, exposed rafter ends, and brackets. The wide dormers that break the broad sweep of the roofline and the semi-detached kitchen are also distinctive Craftsman-style features. The picturesque, organic nature of the shingles covering the facade, in large expanses, exhibits the influence of late-nineteenth-century Shingle-style homes on the island.

Bungalow interiors reflect an informal lifestyle. Typically, ceiling heights are low, rooms are of modest size and generally in an open plan, and the main focus is on the living areas, with less space devoted to the bedrooms and kitchen. A common interior feature, as can be seen at 2 Hinckley Lane and 55 Easton Street (FIGURE 5), is simple woodwork consisting of vertical wood battens placed directly against the wall and capped with a horizontal batten or plate rail, creating the effect of more expensive wood paneling.[19] In addition, built-ins are a common and important element in bungalow interiors as they supplant the need for a lot of furniture[20] and help create the "harmony of life indoors" sought by builders of that style. For instance, the bungalows at 47 and 55 Easton Street have built-in cupboards in the dining rooms, and narrow, built-in, recessed window seats (FIGURE 6) off the living rooms that serve as integral components of the rooms.[21]

Nantucketers were still advertising the island as a health resort in the early 1900s, and in designing bungalows there was an almost obsessive interest in healthfulness.[22] For example, hardwood floors were installed as they were easy to maintain and less likely than carpeting to attract dust and germs. Multiple windows and doors and open-plan interiors provided good ventilation. A particularly good example of the latter is 2 Hinckley Lane, which has a spacious living area and a particularly large number of multipaned windows (which were precursors to the picture window).

Featuring a return to fine craftsmanship in the design and building of homes, the bungalow style of architecture became popular during the Arts

{ OPPOSITE }
FIGURE 4: 2 Hinckley Lane. *Craftsman bungalows like "The Last Resort," built in the 1920s, were orientated toward nature and rustic simplicity.*

{ OPPOSITE }
FIGURE 5: Bungalow
Dining Room, Built in
1914, 55 Easton.

{ RIGHT }
FIGURE 6: Window Seat,
55 Easton Street.

and Crafts movement in America, which advocated a revival of handcrafted furniture, objects, and architecture. The movement was a revolt against an increasingly industrialized society and the mass production of goods. On Nantucket, the spread of the Arts and Crafts aesthetic in the early decades of the twentieth century was due in part to the influence of the Coffin School. Upon the recommendation of the artist Elizabeth Rebecca Coffin (1850–1930), in 1903 the school began to offer classes in manual training (woodworking, metalworking, and basketry) to public schoolchildren, as well as evening classes in advanced woodworking for adults. Students learned the principles of craftsmanship and made furniture and objects in the Arts and Crafts style.[23] Photographs of the school's interior from about 1904 (FIGURE 7) show handcrafted furniture being made, and the school's library owned the Radford Architectural Company series of design books for bungalows and other "modern" styles of building. In the early 1900s, Coffin School girls even sewed "bungalow aprons and caps," apparel considered suitable to cozy bungalow life.

    In building bungalows Nantucket was following a national trend; by 1920 "bungalow mania" had permeated much of America's suburban landscape, and the bungalow was the most popular and fashionable smaller house in the country. Nonresident property owners outnumbered island resident own-

FIGURE 7: Coffin School Interior, ca. 1905. *Early-twentieth-century bungalows were often furnished with Arts and Crafts–style furniture. The Coffin School on Winter Street offered classes in this style and helped spread the Arts and Crafts aesthetic across the island.* Courtesy of the Nantucket Historical Association.

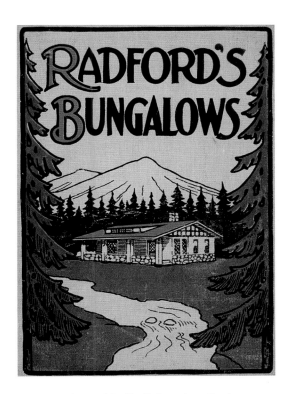

FIGURE 8: Cover of Radford's Bungalows Catalog, 1908. *The bungalow style spread across the country and to Nantucket Island through mail-order catalogs, like the series published by the Radford Architectural Company in Chicago, Illinois.*

ers by a large margin in the early 1920s,[24] therefore it is not surprising that the prevalent style was brought to the island and appeared in growing numbers. The bungalow offered enterprising builders and suppliers an easily standardized and aesthetically appealing house type. The style was promoted through advertisements and articles in national periodicals, combined with the publishing of house-plan books. Many articles created further demand for the style by promising consumers a new, improved domestic life with the purchase of a bungalow.[25] Products were merchandised specifically for the bungalow market across the country; on Nantucket advertisements in the local paper offered "bungalow porch shades," "bungalow aprons," "wool fiber rugs for the bungalow," and "bungalow beds."[26]

A large number of bungalows were built on Easton Street and the surrounding neighborhood leading up to Brant Point. The first were constructed in the 1910s when the area was still very rural, with unpaved roads and unobstructed views of the waterfront. The bungalow style was intensely marketed across the country through mail-order catalogs, which enticed buyers with glowing descriptions, handsome illustrations, and reasonable costs (FIGURE 8). They sold house plans, as well precut lumber and detailing labeled for easy assembly by local labor.[27] Some companies even provided financing for homeowners. Among the companies whose kit homes appear to have been built on Nantucket are Aladdin; Sears, Roebuck & Co.; Lewis Manufacturing Company; Gordon-Van Tine; the Radford Architectural Company; and the Kenyon Take-Down Houses. The latter, a company in Wisconsin, advertised in the Nantucket *Inquirer and Mirror*, in 1912, complete houses "artistic, practical, inexpensive, ideal for summer service" with hardwood floors, awnings, screen doors, and between one and five rooms, for the price of $42 to $320.[28]

Although most of the catalogue homes on the island have changed considerably and are difficult to identify, the bungalow at 55 Easton Street, called Windward (FIGURE 9), is clearly house design number 7067-B in Radford's 1908 catalogue *Artistic Bungalows* (FIGURE 10).[29] The facade of Windward is almost identical and the interior has the exact same footprint as the published plans (FIGURE 11).[30] When Windward was built in 1914 as a summer rental property, an advertisement was placed in the *Inquirer and*

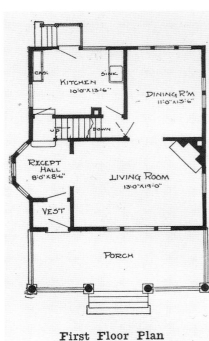

First Floor Plan

{ OPPOSITE }

FIGURE 9: Windward, 55 Easton Street. *Built in 1914, Windward was one of the first mail-order bungalows to be built in the Brant Point area.*

{ TOP }

FIGURE 10: House Design No. 7067-B, in *Radford's Artistic Bungalows* (New York: The Radford Architectural Company, 1908; reprinted by Dover Publications, Inc., New York, 1997), 64.

{ BOTTOM }

FIGURE 11: First-floor Plans, House Design No. 7067-B, in *Radford's Artistic Bungalows* (New York: The Radford Architectural Company, 1908; reprinted by Dover Publications, Inc., New York, 1997), 64.

FIGURE 12: Twin Hollys, 47 Easton Street.
*Built about 1915, this bungalow is notable for
its cozy porch with cobblestone supports.*

FIGURE 13: Detail of Porch, Twin Hollys.

Mirror touting its amenities: "Fully furnished, hardwood floors, electric lights, sanitary plumbing, hot and cold water, open fire-place, broad piazza, butler's pantry, telephone—every modern convenience...location commands a fine view of Nantucket harbor and is within easy access of the steamboat landing, the hotels and bathing beach."[31]

Another example of a catalog bungalow is 47 Easton Street, Twin Hollys (FIGURES 12, 13), which appears to be an expanded version of The Sylvan, published in the 1925 catalogue of the Lewis Manufacturing Company of Bay City, Michigan.[32] Like the Sylvan, Twin Hollys has a full-width front porch, a hip roof that supports dormer windows, rustic cobblestone porch supports capped by wood posts, a stone chimney, and porch parapets that match the shingled walls of the house. Like Craftsman-style bungalows, 47 Easton Street emphasizes structural elements in the design. From the street, the front porch is the feature that most defines it, with its cool shadows offering shelter from the blazing summer sun.

In recent years authentic bungalows have become much sought after by Arts and Crafts enthusiasts, and are increasingly recognized as a significant type of architecture that should be preserved. There is a magazine devoted to the subject, as well as numerous new books and reprints of old mail-order catalogs that explore its merits. In the mid-1920s, however, some Nantucket summer visitors criticized the style. Hermann Hagedorn, a New Yorker and summer resident of Quaise, represented a group of summer residents at the Board of Selectmen's meeting in September 1925, and protested that the bungalows being built on Easton Street were not in keeping with island architecture and "not at all pleasing to the eye."[33] He warned that the "bungalow bug" or "invasion of cheap architecture" was threatening the island's quaintness.[34] In a letter to the editor he explained, "The bungalow disease is worse than the chestnut blight or a forest fire for ruining the looks of a landscape. Let us pray by night and strive by day that the bug make no further headway in Nantucket. Your town is too rare and beautiful . . . to be permitted in its prime to fall a victim to bungalow-itis."[35] Hagedorn was particularly disgusted by the catalog homes, writing that "Anyone who builds one of the ornate, fuzzy-wuzzy, mail-order contraptions, such as have recently begun to appear on the island, in effect endows

and perpetuates what amounts to a public nuisance."[36]

Despite these protests, bungalows continued to be popular on the island, built to meet the increased demand for summer accommodations and as an economical choice for islanders of modest means. In the mid- to late 1920s quite a few bungalows were built in the neighborhood of Five Corners, on York Street and Atlantic Avenue, which is traditionally a working-class community featuring moderate-sized homes and small businesses. Among the bungalows at Five Corners is 37 York Street, built circa 1929–30 for Edith and Joseph Perry, both of Cape Verdean descent and year-round residents of the island.[37]

{ OPPOSITE }

FIGURE 14: Stone Fireplace, Nantucket Bungalow. *This rustic, natural stone fireplace with cement mantel and adjoining built-in seating nook is typical of Craftsman-style bungalows. It was constructed by Byron E. Pease and Edward G. Thomas in 1912 as a rental cottage in the Brant Point area. Fireplaces like this were the main focal point of the living room—a symbol of the "hearth and home" cult associated with bungalow living.*

{ ABOVE }

FIGURE 15: 20 Milk Street, Built ca. 1938. *Once a popular house form on Nantucket, especially for middle-class families summering or living on the island, the modest-sized bungalow and its place in the island's streetscape is a topic of much debate among island homeowners and preservationists today.*

Today, bungalows continue to serve the island as cozy retreats for numerous visitors and residents, but their place in the island's streetscape is a topic of debate, much as it was in the 1920s. In a recent controversy over the fate of an aging bungalow at 20 Milk Street (FIGURE 15) local preservation authorities advocated saving the building and keeping it on its original site, indicating that it is an integral part of the neighborhood. However, the recent owner of the bungalow and neighbors feel it is unsightly and not in keeping with the "quaint" historic styles of eighteenth- and nineteenth-century Nantucket architecture; they advocate instead its demolition or relocation.[38] In this age of enormous "trophy" houses,[39] the bungalow—with middle-class origins, modest size, and practicality—has less appeal for some. As the discussions over the fate of 20 Milk Street continue, it becomes clear just how intensely passionate Nantucketers are about their architecture. The charming little bungalow, although not embraced by everyone, is a reminder of less opulent times, and is indeed a significant part of the island's architectural history.

From Scallop Shanty to Studio:
Artists Transform Old Structures

MARGARET MOORE BOOKER

Water's Edge, Art Studio, ca. 1930s. *One of the many old fishing shanties along the waterfront in Nantucket that was converted into an artist's studio in the 1920s.* Courtesy of the Nantucket Historical Association.

IN THE EARLY 1920S, a thriving artists' colony was established along Nantucket's picturesque harbor front. The establishment of the colony was largely due to Florence Lang (1862–1943), an amateur artist, generous patron of the arts, and summer resident from Montclair, New Jersey. In 1923 she renovated an odd assortment of creaky old shingled shacks, mainly in the Commercial Wharf (now Swain's Wharf) area, into artists' studios. An old forge, an abandoned railroad station, a sail-loft, a candle factory, a slaughterhouse, and scallop and fish shanties were converted into studio apartments with kitchenettes and other modern conveniences and were rented out to artists for a low fee each summer. A writer for the *Boston Herald* claimed that Lang's studios made Nantucket "a paradise and dream come true" for artists, and were attracting to the island "men and women of achievement in the artist world."[1] The writer explained, "Think of a studio apartment, kitchenette, bath and big studio—for the sum of $70 for the season! Think of others to be had even for $50—and then realize why Nantucket artists are still rubbing their eyes and wondering if it's really true!"

As exhibition venues were important to the growth of the colony, Lang also renovated a candle house on Commercial Wharf—where spermaceti candles were manufactured in the nineteenth century—into a gallery. Later, she purchased and moved a saltwater bathhouse (formerly a cooper's shop) from South Beach to Easy Street, where it was opened in 1924 as a gallery.

Lang's renovations inspired other visiting artists to convert historic properties into studios and galleries. One of the more unusual instances is a building called "Greater Light" on Howard Street.[2] In 1932–33, Gertrude and Hanna Monaghan, two artistic Quakers from Pennsylvania, converted a dilapidated, weather-beaten, late-eighteenth-century barn into a summer residence with living space and studio. The sisters retained the overall integrity of the shingled saltbox, but tastefully adorned the exterior and interior with an eclectic array of decorative arts and architectural fragments collected from around the world. Casement windows with amber-colored bottle glass and wrought-iron balconettes are among the interesting features still seen on the exterior today.

At least one island realtor/contractor, Walter I. Brock, took advantage of the thriving artists' colony on Nantucket and in 1923–24 developed a scheme called Greenwich Village on two acres of land on Sunset Hill, facing North Liberty Street. Only those homebuyers who could "do something clever, paint, write, sing, golf, ride, swim or bridge" were "welcomed to Greenwich and the simple life."[3] Obviously named after the artistic community in New York City, Brock's village was to consist of "small artistic homes, with small artistic gardens, at small artistic cost, situated on the highest point in the town, with a wonderful view of the famous Italian Sunsets for which Nantucket is so famous."[4] Purchasers of the lots, which ranged in price from $300 to $350, were required to build an inexpensive artistic bungalow or studio and provide landscaping and a moderately priced summer home for families of modest means. Two small cottages from the scheme still exist today, tucked away on a hilltop, at 55 and 57 North Liberty Street. They are simple, single-story, shingled cottages and remnants of the island's early artists' colony.

1. Reprinted as "Real Artists' Paradise Found on Nantucket Island," in the I&M, 22 September 1923.
2. Owned by the Nantucket Historical Association, this building was called "Greater Light" by the Monaghan sisters. The name derives from the biblical verse "And God made two lights, the greater light to rule the day and the lesser light to rule the night; and he made the stars also."
3. I&M, 11 August 1923.
4. I&M, 21 July 1923.

CHAPTER 7

Twentieth-Century Design

Patricia Egan Butler

SINCE early building traditions and customs have evolved into strict design review and regulation for all new structures, significant examples of modernism, postmodernism, and contemporary architecture are rare on Nantucket. Colonial Revivals of the 1920s, pre-1940 Craftsman bungalows, and post-1950 contemporary "deck houses" do exist on Nantucket, but until the building boom in the 1980s, more attention was given to the restoration of old houses than to new construction. New buildings tended to be simple gabled forms, derivative and consistent, covered with white cedar shingles, and adhering to accepted formulas.

However, some twentieth-century architects and architectural designers have created innovative homes that are in keeping with the island's heritage of excellent design. Distinguished contemporary island architecture is guided by the past, but does not follow it. Architectural historian Vincent Scully expresses this eloquently when writing about the Trubeck and Wislocki houses (FIGURE 1). Designed with history, building tradition, and originality by the Philadelphia-based architects Robert Venturi and John Rauch, with the assistance of Terry Vaughan, these houses were built in 1971–72 at Pocomo, a peninsula extending into Pocomo Harbor four miles east of Nantucket Town.

When describing the Trubeck and Wislocki houses, Scully wrote, "Venturi creates a totally different and equally valid image of America, of the empty horizon, the lonely island, and the Viking sea. In doing so he makes direct use not only of the placement of the Greek temples at Selinunte, but also of the American tradition of wooden houses and especially and most consciously of the Shingle Style. But now the houses stand up, very tense, very taut, and lonely, like individuals trying to speak to each other, Americans in their predicament here."[1]

Unfortunately the open landscape context that inspired this passage no longer exists. Pocomo Point has been built up, with sprawling, stretched out, multi-gabled variations of a house type that has proliferated on Nantucket's outlying areas, which are not protected by conservation restrictions.

{ OPPOSITE }
FIGURE 1: One of the Trubeck and Wislocki Houses, Pocomo, Built in 1971–72. *Designed by Robert Venturi and John Rauch, with the assistance of Terry Vaughan.*

A year before the Trubeck and Wislocki houses, a contemporary condominium development called Tristram's Landing (FIGURE 2) was built in Madaket. The construction of the attached units was flimsy and unsuitable for island weather conditions. Plate-glass windows, decks, atypical roof massing, and overall indifference to building tradition in Tristram's Landing prompted the community to extend the jurisdiction of its Historic District Commission to encompass the whole island.

The extension of the HDC's authority required creating design standards to apply to new construction beyond the "old and historic districts." The commission eventually hired J. Christopher Lang to write *Building With Nantucket in Mind*, which was published in 1978.[2] A graduate of Preservation Institute: Nantucket, a highly regarded summer program affiliated with the University of Florida, Lang pointed out that beginning in the 1960s, single-family residences on large lots began to overwhelm the island's open spaces. By interpreting the understated simplicity of the past and working with the physical and natural qualities of the land, Lang suggested that new construction could complement rather than detract from the island's fragile beauty.

Contemporary design excellence on Nantucket faces community planning challenges. The island's zoning regulations were established at the same time the HDC's jurisdiction was extended. However, the adopted zoning measures followed typical suburban models and resulted in the island's open areas being devoured by its own version of sprawl—large parcels of land with oversized houses. Nantucket's planning board depends on the zoning by-laws, but has no corresponding subdivision design guidebook and relies on the HDC to address the impact of new construction.

FIGURE 2: Tristram's Landing. *Built in the 1960s, Tristram's Landing is a development of attached dwellings near the village of Madaket that brought about legislation to include the entire island under the jurisdiction of the Nantucket Historic District Commission.*

FIGURE 3: The Gamble House on Pocomo Point. *A postmodern style of architecture designed in 1989 by architect Travis Price.*

{ RIGHT }
FIGURE 4: Innishail on Cliff Road. *The 1875 Colonial Revival/Shingle Style home that inspired the design of the Gamble House on Pocomo Point.*

Previous chapters have pointed out that historically Nantucket's architecture has been differentiated by what is best described as harmony, which brings all the island's buildings together, both aesthetically and in spirit. New design should also be harmonious and integrated, whether the context is town, village, or outlying areas.

The people who live on Nantucket have a keen and prideful sense of place, and the community is immersed with knowledge about the island's buildings and their history. Long-time residents' knowledge comes from a lifetime of visual understanding and practical application. Recent arrivals come with appreciation for the island's unique building tradition and soon develop their own loyalty to the community's customs and society. For all Nantucketers the official work of the HDC may be thought of as a formalization of traditional architectural customs meant to preserve the aesthetic spirit of the past.

Harmony became the issue when a postmodern design by architect Travis Price was built in 1989 on a prominent site on a high bluff overlooking Pocomo Harbor (FIGURE 3). At that time, the HDC primarily consisted of architects or designers who yearned to break away from repetitive applications of look-alike capes, upside-down saltboxes, and ill-proportioned boxes with multiple "dog-house" dormers—blueprints that addressed the guidelines, but that fell far short of representing the spirit of Nantucket's architecture. Price, who had previous commissions on Nantucket and a versatile architectural practice in Takoma Park, Maryland, was accomplished in a broad range of projects, from historic restorations to contemporary designs. After driving his clients around the island looking at houses that might inspire their own design, Innishail, a turn-of-the-century Shingle-style house on Cliff Road (FIGURE 4) was chosen as the model. Price interpreted the gambrel rooflines and Colonial Revival details of Innishail imaginatively into a playful postmodern look, including an oversized broken pediment entry, atypical execution of detail, and extenuated window shapes placed asymmetrically on the facade. However, when applied to massing on a grand scale on the prominent Pocomo site, the overall composition prompted community concern. In April of 1991, after months of photographs, articles, and letters to the newspaper, two members of the Historic District Commission were voted off the commission and replaced by more conventional islanders.[3]

FIGURE 5: Late Twentieth-Century Houses in Cisco, 1998. *Overview of a large-lot sub-division on the south shore.*

Depending on one's point of view, the community's reaction to postmodern design reflected an architectural tradition that was spirited, proud, and in control. Or, as others thought, Nantucket's long tradition of evolving architectural excellence was doomed.

Economic recession further limited contemporary design concerns until the mid-1990s, when Nantucket came into its own as a destination resort and property values soared. Some houses built around this time looked like mini-hotels programmed for corporate entertaining rather than for family needs. Oriented to capture ocean views, stretched-out, two-story massing prototypes occupy every square foot of allowed footprint, with little relationship to each other or to their landscape (FIGURE 5).

But there are exceptions. As in the past, historic reference combined with scale, context, simplicity, and craftsmanship are key elements for excellent new design on Nantucket. Architect Graham Gund's family residence, built in 1994 near Washing Pond (named because early settlers washed sheep in the pond before shearing), reflects all of these elements (FIGURES 6, 7). A stone's throw from the site of the original settlement of Sherburne near Capaum Pond, the house is situated on a high bluff that borders sweeping open moorland, presently owned and maintained for public use by the Nantucket Conservation Foundation.

In addition to award-winning new residential, commercial, and academic architectural projects, Gund is noted for his far-reaching historic preservation and urban development interests. In Massachusetts, his work in Newburyport, the restorations of several buildings at Bullfinch Square in Boston, and the Williston Library at Mount Holyoke College contributed to his election as trustee of the National Trust for Historic Preservation.

Gund's Nantucket house is a blend of innovation, historical influences, and careful attention to the community's design review requirements. "The concept of buildings being added over time

{ CLOCKWISE FROM TOP }
FIGURE 6: The Gund
House from Tupancy
Links (A Nantucket
Conservation Foundation
Property), 1997. Photograph
by Patricia Egan Butler.

FIGURE 7. The Gund
House Near Washing
Pond, North Shore, Built
in 1994. Photograph by Peter
Aaron/Esto.

FIGURE 8: Interior of the
Gund House. Photograph by
Peter Aaron/Esto.

shaped my design. This gives the place an organic form and lends a casual feel to the buildings in this pastoral setting," Gund commented in a 1996 article written by Brendan Gill.[4] The concept of additive massing is a long-held New England (and Nantucket) rural building practice. Typically, first the main farmhouse was built, then the barn, followed by a back ell on the house and additional sheds and outbuildings. All of these were gathered around an inner, protected "dooryard," the center of activity back and forth between the buildings and the fields beyond. At the Gund house the central open space functions as driveway and courtyard. Gill wrote that the interior of the Gund house has gables that are "supported by scissorslike beams...that seem to miss each other playfully as they pass, like gulls in flight" (FIGURE 8).[5] The house was designed for family and friends' comfort and enjoyment of the light, air, and views of the ocean and the moors. The landscaping features sturdy indigenous plants, grasses, and shrubs, in keeping with the weathered white cedar shingles and the unpretentious structures of the home: porches, roof walks, and rose trellises, which all use the vocabulary of the past with knowing inventiveness.

FIGURE 9: The Ellis House, Built in 1995. *A contemporary design in Quaise Pastures on Pocomo Harbor, by Christopher F. Holland.*

FIGURE 10: The Hudson Home, Built in 1992. *Architectural designer Brook Meerbergen's expansion of a one-room cottage on Halyard Lane in the Pine Valley subdivision.* Photograph by Patricia Egan Butler.

Excellent contemporary design can be attributed to on-island architects and architectural designers as well. Architect Christopher F. Holland studied at the University of Virginia School of Architecture and has lived on island for thirty-nine years. His work is known for its innately appropriate scale and complementary relationship to site topography and vegetation. In a house he built in 1995 in Quaise on Polpis Harbor (FIGURE 9), Holland gave great attention to an overall low massing, facing south on a gentle rise. A muted palette is respectful of surrounding nature. A rural historic reference is provided by the cupola. Holland's subtle and appealing architecture is contemporary, yet firmly informed by Nantucket's building customs.

Brook Meerbergen grew up on Nantucket and after studying economics at the University of Connecticut returned to the island to apprentice with Milton Rowland. Rowland is perhaps best known for designs that reflect his own affinity for Nantucket, particularly the late-nineteenth- and early-twentieth-century summer cottages built in Brant Point, where his own family vacationed. Rowland's eye for roof lines, siting, detail, proportion, and window types renders the cottage form

FIGURE 11: The Hall House, Remodeled in 1998. *Architectural designer Mark Avery's interpretive design on Meadow Lane.*

with familiar, yet fresh perspective. Meerbergen's design for expanding a tiny cottage exemplifies the benefits of the self-taught school of architecture (FIGURE 10).

The renovation in 1998 of a nondescript 1960s house on Meadow Lane (FIGURE 11), at the edge of Nantucket Town's old historic district, shows the creative possibilities of working with an existing structure and community design guidelines. The transformed residence relates to early island house types, the late-nineteenth-century Shingle style, and finally, it is an unmistakably fine expression of its own time and place. Both the architectural designer of the house, Mark Avery, and the owner were well versed and dedicated HDC members. The Meadow Lane house points out the potential for all who are given the opportunity to work with Nantucket's buildings, old, recent, or new; grand or ordinary. If design guidelines are thoughtfully married to historic understanding, the spirit of Nantucket's architecture will continue to thrive.

Historic Preservation on Nantucket

PATRICIA EGAN BUTLER

North Liberty Street. Photograph by Gregory Spaid.

IN THE 1950S, businessman and preservationist Walter Beinecke, Jr. revisited the island haunt of his youth with an ambitious economic development plan. At that time, the Nantucket waterfront was severely impoverished, little was left of the fishing industry, and the core historic district was languishing. In an effort to change this situation, Beinecke established the Nantucket Historical Trust and Sherburne Associates. He then bought dozens of historic residential and commercial properties, began restoring the downtown and the wharves, and generally infused the dormant summer resort with attractions geared toward wealthy vacationers.

Beinecke's work was coincident with increased national historic preservation awareness. Recognizing the aesthetic, business, and political opportunities related to the preservation movement, he convinced community leaders to support official historic district legislation. The result was that in 1955 the Nantucket Historic District Commission (HDC) was approved at Town Meeting.

Initially limited to the core historic districts of Nantucket Town and the village of Siasconset, the HDC used past observations to guide its work. The research of historian Everett U. Crosby on Nantucket's architectural heritage—its vulnerability and its importance to the island's economy—was particularly helpful. The 1944 edition of his book, *95% Perfect*, concludes with the *Basic Specifications for Additions and Alterations to the Exterior of Old Nantucket Houses*. In his 1951 pamphlet, *Our Gold Mine: The Dollars Value of the Remaining Oldness of Nantucket Town*, he recommended a voluntary community effort to preserve the town's "remaining oldness through cooperative action, to keep this subject steadily before us, to come promptly to a realization of the danger of soon losing our inheritance."

Eleven years after the Historic District legislation was enacted in 1955, the Department of the Interior, noting 2,400 historic structures, designated Nantucket Island a National Historic Landmark, a recognition only awarded to properties of outstanding national significance.[1]

Up until the 1980s, more attention was given to the restoration of old houses than to new construction on Nantucket, where contractors and builders were skilled in preservation work. By the mid-1990s, however, there was increased interest in Nantucket that imposed overwhelming challenges. Historic preservationists on Nantucket reacted by joining together in 1999 to form the Nantucket Preservation Alliance, composed of sixteen historic, preservation, and educational public and private organizations prepared to address preservation issues. The Nantucket Preservation Trust was established in 1997 as the only year-round nonprofit historic preservation organization dedicated to educational and informational initiatives. In 2000, the island community was surprised when Nantucket earned the dubious distinction of being listed on the National Trust for Historic Preservation's "Eleven Most Endangered Historic Places." "Gut-rehabs" with insensitive replacement materials, and the overall tremendous pressure of inappropriate development within the historic sections and in the outlying areas, were cited as some of the immediate concerns.[2] In fact, Nantucket was characterized as a National Trust "poster child," representing many similarly affected historic places along the East Coast.

A great deal has been accomplished on Nantucket since then. In addition to the efforts of the Nantucket Preservation Alliance, Nantucket Preservation Trust, and other organizations, the Commonwealth of Massachusetts approved the Community Preservation Act (CPA) in 2001. Funding provided by the CPA for open space, affordable housing, and historic preservation is an essential resource for all historic preservation interests, including bricks and mortar projects, and educational programs.

Despite some setbacks—such as the demolition of the 1875 Monument Square Grocery store at 106 Main Street in August of 2001—concerned Nantucketers continue to make preservation an important issue.

1. State Register of Historic Places, National Park Service, U.S. Department of the Interior, Massachusetts Historical Commission, 2001, 191.
2. Rozhon, Tracie, "Nantucket Worries That its Past is Being Renovated Away," *The New York Times*, August 1, 1999, 1.

Notes

ABBREVIATIONS USED IN THE NOTES
Sources frequently cited have been identified by the following abbreviations:

NHA   Manuscript Collection of the Nantucket Historical Association Research Library, Nantucket, Massachusetts.

HABS   Library of Congress, Prints and Photographs Division, Historic American Buildings Survey, Washington, D.C.

I&M   Nantucket *Inquirer and Mirror* newspaper

Note: most misspellings from eighteenth- and nineteenth-century texts were left uncorrected for the sake of authenticity.

INTRODUCTION, PAGES 1–17

1. Edward K. Godfrey, *The Island of Nantucket, What It Was and What It Is* (Boston: Lee and Shepard, Publishers, 1882), 12–13.
2. These numbers were determined by the National Park Service in 1966, when they made the entire island a historic landmark.
3. Joseph Sansom, "A Description of Nantucket," *The Port Folio*, vol. 5 (1811), 38.
4. Vincent Scully, *American Architecture and Urbanism* (New York: Praeger Publishers, 1969), 83–84.
5. The article discusses the merit of the island's architecture and people for artists looking for new subject matter to paint. See P., "Country Correspondence," *The Crayon*, vol. 5 (September 1858), 269.
6. Anonymous, "Nantucket," *The Living Age* vol. 14, no. 172 (August 28, 1847), 402.
7. I&M, 17 March, 1883.
8. Letter to the editor from Alexander Starbuck, I&M, 15 August 1874.
9. "Nantucket as a Place of Resort," Nantucket *Inquirer*, 18 August 1847.
10. William F. Macy, *The Story of Old Nantucket* (Boston: Houghton Mifflin Company, second edition, 1928), 145–146.
11. Letter to the Editor, from "R," I&M, 3 April 1886.
12. "'Sconset," I&M, 25 April 1885.
13. Dona Brown, *Inventing New England: Regional Tourism in the Nineteenth Century* (Washington: Smithsonian Institution, 1995), 106.
14. Ibid., 107.
15. "Old Houses," I&M, 3 September 1881.
16. "July 1895 Nantucket Historical Association's First Annual Meeting," *Historic Nantucket* 43, no. 2 (Summer 1994), 5.
17. "Nantucket's Experiment," I&M, 13 August 1938; originally published in the Tiverton, Rhode Island, *Sentinel*.
18. "Williamsburg and Nantucket," I&M, 24 July 1937; reprint, NHA blue files. Everett U. Crosby, *95% Perfect* (Nantucket, Mass.: Everett U. Crosby, 1937).
19. James C. Massey, "Introduction," in Clay Lancaster's *The Architecture of Historic Nantucket* (New York: McGraw-Hill Book Company, 1972), x.

CHAPTER 1: HEARTH AND HOME, PAGES 18–43

1. Architectural historian Clay Lancaster (1917–2000) explored and catalogued Nantucket's historic buildings and houses in his excellent book, *The Architecture of Historic Nantucket* (New York: McGraw-Hill Book Company, 1972). The authors are indebted to him for the guidance his work has provided.
2. Nathaniel Philbrick's *Away Off Shore: Nantucket Island and Its People, 1602–1890* (Nantucket, Mass.: Mill Hill Press, 1994) was particularly helpful in providing the historical background on the first English inhabitants.
3. For more information on the Wampanoags, see Nathaniel Philbrick's *Abram's Eyes: The Native American Legacy of Nantucket Island* (Nantucket, Mass.: Mill Hill Press, 1998).
4. In 1690, Ichabod Paddock, a whaleman from Cape Cod, was recruited to provide instruction in the hunt. During the seventeenth century, a village on the eastern shore of the island was established as a fishing and whaling outpost. The houses built in the village are discussed in Chapter 5.
5. These early structures were timber frame

construction and therefore were probably fairly easy to disassemble and relocate. Also, houses were often moved whole. Several Nantucket historians have written on the incidence of houses moved from the original settlement near Capaum Pond (1661–1717) to the present location of town. See Henry B. Worth's, *Nantucket Land and Landowners* (Nantucket, Mass.: Nantucket Historical Association, Vol. II, Bulletin No. 5, 1906, reissued 1928), 257.

6. The seventeenth-century timber situation has been broadly debated by Nantucket historians. Henry C. Forman had a plausible and objective view concerning the possibility and proof of existing lumber and the record of importing it. See Henry Forman's *Early Nantucket and Its Whale Houses* (Nantucket, Mass.: Mill Hill Press, second edition, 1991), 26.

7. NHA, Coll. 10, AB 422.

8. Most Nantucket historians have referred to the early houses as medieval in style. However, Marcus Whiffen, a professor and respected authority of American architectural history, states, "When it comes to domestic architecture in the English colonies in the seventeenth century, the epithets Gothic and Medieval should be used with more caution than some writers have exercised." See Whiffen's *American Architecture Since 1780* (Cambridge, Mass.: The MIT Press, 1969), 4.

9. "The plan developed particularly well in East Anglia [a south eastern region of England] during the seventeenth century and the baffle entry arrangement crossed the Atlantic with the colonists and formed the basis for one strand in the web of American vernacular architecture." R. W. Brunskill, *Traditional Buildings of Britain: An Introduction to Vernacular Architecture* (London: Victor Gollancz Ltd., 1992), 53.

10. The massive chimney stack is also characteristic: it rises from partway along the ridge then usually forms a base for separate stacks,

each flue serving a single fireplace until they unite again with a chimney cap which is often highly decorated. R. W. Brunskill, *Traditional Buildings of Britain*, 53.

11. Unless otherwise noted, information on the dates of houses, their original owners, and ownership genealogy are taken from the Library of Congress, Prints and Photographs Division, Historic American Buildings Survey. Information gathered by the University of Florida's Preservation Institute: Nantucket was also helpful in dating houses. Most of the HABS surveys and the PI:N reports are in the library of the NHA.

12. In 1928, the house was moved five hundred feet from its original site where it was in use as a carriage house. Original post and beams were retained, as was the unusual arch molding over the front door. The batten door, casement windows, and chimney are all replacements [but their style is expressive of the original]. HABS, MASS,10-NANT, 55.

13. For further description of the evolution of colonial architecture, see Virginia and Lee McAlester, *A Field Guide to American Houses* (New York: Alfred A. Knopf, 1995), 105.

14. Eighteenth-century use of the word *lean-to* is noted in the will of William Gayer from 1710. Gayer states, "I give to Africa a negro once my servant . . . my now dwelling house and half the leanto and all the other half of my barn . . . during his natural life." NHA, Gayer Family Papers, Coll. 156, Fold. 2.

15. Reported to have been lost at sea in 1725, Captain Gardner did not have a long stay in the house his father, Richard Gardner Jr., is said to have built for him. HABS, MASS,10-NANT,17.

16. The Charles Gardner house is an early baffle-entry design built with a full two-story front and rear (a design that was from the mainland) or perhaps the rear was raised, as suggested by Lancaster. For construction date and further information, see Henry B. Worth, *Nantucket Lands and Landowners*

(Bowie, Md.: Heritage Books, Inc., 1901, facsimile reprint, 1992), 265.

17. Coleman's "A Testimony Against the Practice of Making Slaves of Men" is said to be one of the earliest tracts against slavery published in New England. For further information see NHA Coll. 107, Fold. 9. See also Robert Leach and Peter Gow, *Quaker Nantucket: The Religious Community Behind the Whaling Empire* (Nantucket, Mass.: Mill Hill Press, 1997), 40.

18. Forman, *Early Nantucket and Its Whale Houses*, 243.

19. For more information on the founding families of Nantucket see Worth, *Nantucket Lands and Landowners*.

20. For a comprehensive study of the Friends on Nantucket see Leach and Gow, *Quaker Nantucket*.

21. HABS, MASS, 10-NANT, 55. See also "Starbuck-Kilvert House," unpublished typescript, vol. II, 1980, no. 54, University of Florida, Preservation Institute: Nantucket, NHA.

22. "Swain-Gaylord House," unpublished typescript, vol. I, 1978, no. 25, University of Florida, Preservation Institute: Nantucket, NHA.

23. Most Nantucket historians essentially agree that the features did not exist. Clay Lancaster suggests that the Jethro Coffin house, circa 1686, at Sunset Hill (owned by the NHA), once had facade gables. See Lancaster's *The Architecture of Historic Nantucket*, 21.

24. Lancaster, *The Architecture of Historic Nantucket*, xvi.

25. Carpenter Richard Macy in 1710 noted working on boats in his account book. He recorded, "work about youre boat" for Stephen P[reacher] and in 1715 noted, "mending the long boat" for Jedehiah Fich. NHA, Coll. 10, AB 422.

26. For more information on shipbuilding influences, see Chapter 2, page 73.

27. Architectural historian Everett Crosby relates a story concerning Quaker priorities. "When a certain house near Stone Alley was being erected from frames made

on the mainland, it was found to be upright all around, the back two stories high like the front and so without the regulation long back roof. To some of the Islanders this caused uneasiness, as being likely to introduce change and extravagance. A citizen's meeting was convened and the owner requested to cut down the back posts. Good man as he was, he complied." Everett U. Crosby, *95% Perfect* (Nantucket, Mass.: Inquirer and Mirror Press, 1944), 26.

28. I am grateful to J. Edward Hood, research historian, Old Sturbridge Village, for sharing this information with me.

29. Use of the words *chamber* (for bedroom and/or storage room) and *garret* (attic room) are noted in the will of William Gayer from 1710. Gayer states, "I give to my house keeper Patience Foot...the west chamber and garret and half the leanto of my now dwelling house to hold and possess...during her natural life." NHA, Gayer Family Papers. Coll. 156, Fold. 2.

30. Transom lights are typical on both the exterior and interior of a Nantucket house. Interior transoms—without glass early on—were said to be used to detect a fire that may have dangerously flared.

31. On an island of wooden houses, fear of fire was a stressful reality. In addition to the transom lights, shuttles (roof hatches) and roof walks (platforms) were built to quickly gain access to the roof in order to douse a chimney fire.

32. The baffle-entry plan that stopped the wind from sweeping through the house can be compared with the cross-entry design that allowed a breeze through—a plan favored by the colonists in the warm climates of the southern regions of the United States.

33. Lancaster, *The Architecture of Historic Nantucket*, 160.

34. Richard Macy. NHA, Coll. 10, AB 422.

35. Benjamin Newland. NHA, Coll. 10, AB 103.

36. John Coffin. NHA, Coll. 10, AB 518.

37. In the journal of John Richardson, an itinerant Quaker orator who visited the island in 1701, there is recorded an instance where the windows in the house of his hosts (Nathaniel and Mary Starbuck) were removed from their frames. He writes: "the large and bright rubbed Room was set with suitable seats and chairs, the glass windows taken out of the frames, and many chairs placed without very conveniently.... " Removal of the windows allowed the people in the front yard of the house to be able to hear the words of Richardson, who was speaking to a capacity crowd in the Starbuck home. NHA, Coll. 335, Fold. 606.

38. On an island of seamen who often used nautical terms in everyday speech, a "clinker-built" house referred to a construction technique that looked like the external planks of a ship.

39. In 1714, carpenter Richard Macy notes the labor of "bording at thy house" for Joseph [R]usel. Macy may be referring to clapboards. NHA, Coll. 10, AB 518.

40. NHA, Coll. 10, AB 518.

41. NHA, Coll. 10, AB 422.

42. NHA, Coll. 10, AB 103.

43. NHA, Coll. 10, AB 518.

44. "Starbuck-Kilvert House," unpublished typescript, vol. II, 1980, no. 54, University of Florida, Preservation Institute: Nantucket, NHA.

45. Undated newspaper clipping, NHA, coll. 57, Grace Brown Gardner Scrapbooks.

CHAPTER 2: A RELIGIOUS ETHIC, PAGES 44–73

1. The first paragraphs of this chapter are adapted from an article by Rose Gonnella that appeared in *Nantucket Magazine* (Fall 2001).

2. Descended from Edward Starbuck, one of the original purchasers of Nantucket, Joseph Starbuck was an enormously successful whaling merchant. He built three identical Federal-style brick houses for his sons. The houses are situated three in a row on upper Main Street. The story of Joseph's birth appears in Will Gardner's *Three Bricks and Three Brothers: The Story of the Nantucket Whale-Oil Merchant Joseph Starbuck* (Nantucket, Mass: Whaling Museum Publications, 1945), 1.

3. The unusually large, well-preserved chimney is a feature of and clue to the early-eighteenth-century construction date of the house. HABS, MASS #920, 10-NANT, 72.

4. "Greasy luck" refers to the success of whalers who were lucky enough to have brought back to Nantucket hundreds of barrels of valuable whale oil. Nathaniel Philbrick, *Away Off Shore: Nantucket Island and Its People, 1602–1890* (Nantucket, Mass.: Mill Hill Press, 1994), 172.

5. The Society of Friends is the proper (and preferred name) for the Quaker religion. See Robert Leach and Peter Gow, *Quaker Nantucket: The Religious Community Behind the Whaling Empire* (Nantucket, Mass: Mill Hill Press, 1997), ix–x.

6. J. Hector St. John de Crèvecoeur, *Letters from Nantucket and Martha's Vineyard* (Boston: Applewood Books, 1986), 21. Originally, de Crèvecoeur's work was published under the title *Letters from an American Farmer* (London: Thomas Davies, 1782).

7. Leach and Gow, *Quaker Nantucket*, 9.

8. Much has been written on the early social history of the colonists of Nantucket, including their collective efforts to create their own form of government and remain independent of Puritan rule. For further information see chapters 3 and 4 in Philbrick, *Away Off Shore*.

9. Leach and Gow, *Quaker Nantucket*, 30.

10. Leach and Gow, *Quaker Nantucket*, 6.

11. Leach and Gow, *Quaker Nantucket*, 18–19.

12. Leach writes, "consistent Quakers make a point of eschewing signs of deferential formalities and worldly vanity. Plain dress and speech (including the use of the pronouns "thou," "thee," and "thy"—equivalent to the familiar *tu-toi* in French) characterized

some Quaker communities into the twentieth century" (*Quaker Nantucket*, 7).

13. Not all Nantucketers were Friends and therefore not compelled to build houses with the plan recommended. Even Friends did not build according to this directive. Some nonmembers chose the home for practical reasons while others did build outside the Quaker norm. Eventually, many of the Friends broke away from the confining codes of conduct. A dislike of the unyielding and strict order of behavior, in conjunction with other worldly forces tempting the Friends, led to a split among members and the gradual demise of the group. Leach discusses their factious split in the latter half of his book, *Quaker Nantucket*.

14. Four-bay house facades would have three windows and a door on the first floor and four windows on the second.

15. NHA, Coll. 10, AB 214. Misspelled words are taken directly from the carpenters' account books and are left uncorrected throughout this text.

16. Labor on the sloop *Dove* and the ships *Amazone*, *Dauphin*, and *Lydia* were also recorded by Coffin. NHA, Coll. 10, AB 518.

17. See Niles Parker's essay entitled "Ship Shape," page 73.

18. These typical Nantucket houses are catalogued in Clay Lancaster's, *The Architecture of Historic Nantucket* (New York: McGraw-Hill Book Company, 1972).

19. For more information on Georgian-style houses see Virginia and Lee McAlester's, *A Field Guide to American Houses* (New York: Alfred A. Knopf, 1995), 139.

20. The southeast section is said to have been brought from old Sherburne and rebuilt on Centre Street. At that time the rear ell was added. HABS, MASS-920, 10-NANT, 72.

21. The two-and-a half-story (front and rear) style has been labeled a New England farmhouse (of three, four, or five bays) by Lester Walker in his book, *American Homes: The*

Illustrated Encyclopedia of Domestic Architecture (New York: Black Dog & Leventhal Publishers, 1996), 78, and labeled a "preclassical box" by Virginia and Lee McAlester, *A Field Guide to American Houses*, 78. Lancaster places Nantucket's three- and five-bay houses with a central or ridge chimney into a category labeled "late colonial" (*The Architecture of Historic Nantucket*, 73, 250).

22. The style is variably dated between 1720 to 1750s by the historians noted above.

23. Lancaster, *The Architecture of Historic Nantucket*, 250.

24. Most important is not the exact category of the design but the interesting blend of models and the preservation of its varied history.

25. See Chapter 3 for further information on Federal-style houses on Nantucket.

26. HABS, MASS-855, 10-NANT, 20.

27. Elizabeth Crosby (Plaskett) Bennett, edited by her daughter Florence Bennett Anderson, "A Nantucketer Remembers," *Old-Time New England*, vol. XLII, no. 1 (1951), 3.

28. Exact date of the construction of 11 Milk Street needs further research. Deeds are not clear and historians have not completely substantiated the date of 1790. If the house was moved to Milk Street, as suggested in the information provided by a HABS document (MASS #942, 10-NANT, 12), Joseph Starbuck, whose known birthdate is 1774, could not have been born in the house as it stands on Milk Street. For further information see "Thomas Starbuck House," unpublished typescript, 2001, University of Florida, Preservation Institute: Nantucket, NHA.

29. The Starbuck clan lived along Milk Street, a thoroughfare at the junction of Main and Gardner streets. To the southwest corner of the intersection stood the Town House, the meeting place for local governmental affairs. Marie.M. Coffin, HABS, MASS #942, 10-NANT, 12.

30. A good number of lean-tos existed side-by-side with the typical Nantucket house and continued to be built through the 1800s. See Chapter 1.

31. HABS, MASS-932, 10-NANT, 51.f

32. Henry B. Worth, *Nantucket Land and Landowners* (Bowie, Md.: Heritage Books, Inc., Facsimile reprint, 1992), 232.

33. Once known as a "Christian door" on Nantucket, this type of door had six raised panels that form the shape of a cross at the top. At the bottom, the form is reminiscent of an open book, symbolizing a bible. It is known at lumberyards today as a "cross and bible" door.

34. Winders consist of steps carried around curves or angles; also, they are steps with one end of the tread wider than the other end.

35. In addition, not all the houses were owned by Friends; non-Quakers also recognized the practical value of the form. In a reminiscence of her childhood, Elizabeth Crosby (Plaskett) Bennett noted that her Unitarian parents bought a typical Nantucket house because as Elizabeth's mother said, "the house must be one built by honest day's labor, not a jerry contraption." Elizabeth Crosby (Plaskett) Bennett, edited by her daughter Florence Anderson, "A Nantucketer Remembers," *Old-Time New England* vol. XLII, no. 1 (1951), 8.

36. HABS, Mass, 10-NANT, 75A.

37. NHA Coll. 335, Fold. 262.

38. Bennett, "A Nantucketer Remembers," 9.

39. It is not clear whether the decoration was added at the time of construction or at a later date. HABS #1049, 10-NANT, 755.

40. Usually a masonry feature, a quoin is a slightly projecting, decorative block at the corner walls. The wooden quoins on 27 India Street echo the brick and stone decoration found on elaborate Georgian-style homes.

CHAPTER 3:
WHALING PROSPERITY, PAGES 74–107

1. Edouard A. Stackpole, *The Forgotten Man of the Boston Tea Party* (Edouard A. Stackpole, 1973), 11.

2. *I & M*, 1921 Supplement, *100 Years on Nantucket*.

3. George Allen Fowlkes, *A Mirror of Nantucket: An Architectural History of The Island, 1686–1850* (Plainfield, N.J.: Press of Interstate, 1959), 58.

4. William Edward Gardner, *Three Bricks and Three Brothers: The Story of the Nantucket Whale-Oil Merchant* (Cambridge, Mass: Riverside Press, 1945). Colorful narrative about the prominent Starbuck family.

5. Historic American Buildings Survey Number MASS 10-NANT 765: Second Congregational Meeting House. Suggests that the original building had a street-facing gable with a square tower incorporated on the facade ,which in turn was topped by a round tower and weather vane.

6. Alexander Starbuck, *The History of Nantucket: County, Island and Town, Including Genealogies of First Settlers* (Boston: C. E. Goodspeed & Co., 1924; reprint by Charles E. Tuttle Company, Rutland, Vermont, 1969), 559.

7. Clay Lancaster, *Nantucket in the Nineteenth Century* (New York: Dover Publications, Inc., 1979), 43.

8. Talbot Faulkner Hamlin, *Greek Revival Architecture in America* (New York, London & Toronto: Oxford University Press, 1944), 169.

9. Jane E. Crawford "The United Methodist Church," *Historic Nantucket*, vol. 25 (Summer 1977), 24.

10. Henry S. Wyer, *Sea-Girt Nantucket: A Handbook of Historical and Contemporaneous Information for Visitors* (Nantucket, Mass.: Henry S. Wyer, second edition, 1906), 104.

11. In early timber frame construction, a gunstock post is a corner post tapered in the form of a rifle.

12. HABS - HAER MASS No. (unassigned) and Clarissa Penny Porter Family Records.

13. Hamlin, *Greek Revival Architecture in America*.

14. Asher Benjamin, *The American Builder's Companion* (Boston: R. P. & C. Williams, 1827).

15. Asher Benjamin, *The American Builder's Companion* (New York: Unabridged republication, Dover Publications, Inc., 1969), 63.

16. Benjamin, *The American Builder's Companion*, 63.

17. Erwin O. Christensen, *Early American Wood Carving* (New York: Dover Publications, Inc., 1972), 79. "Local variations in the way moldings were cut, and reeding, fluting and gouge work were interpreted. Sometimes the carver may have misunderstood the line drawings of his guide book and inadvertently made a change where he thought he was following the book."

18. Clay Lancaster, *The Architecture of Historic Nantucket* (New York: McGraw-Hill Book Company, 1977), 216.

19. Lancaster, *Nantucket in the Nineteenth Century*, 62.

20. Kenneth Duprey, *Old Houses on Nantucket* (New York: Architectural Book Publishing Co., Inc., 1959), 204.

21. Joseph Q. Knapp, *Nantucket Journal*, 11 February 1892.

22. Advertisements in *Nantucket Mirror*, 10 and 17 October 1838.

23. See chapter 1, endnote 36, this volume.

24. Starbuck, *The History of Nantucket*, 552.

25. Lancaster, *The Architecture of Historic Nantucket*, 143, endnote 6.

26. Calder Loth and Julius Trousdale Sadler Jr., *The Only Proper Style: Gothic Architecture in America*, (Boston: Little, Brown and Company, 1975), 50.

27. Lancaster, *The Architecture of Historic Nantucket*, 116, 218.

28. R. A. Douglas-Lithgow, *Nantucket: A History* (New York: Knickerbocker Press, 1914), 175.

29. Hamlin, *Greek Revival Architecture in America*, 168–169.

30. The school was a private academy with classes initially taught under the then popular Lancasterian method of teaching: using the brightest students as monitors and tutors, with one class teaching what it had learned to the class below.

31. The school's first building was located at the corner of Fair and Lyon streets.

32. An early account book lists the names of several builders/carpenters who were involved in the building of the Coffin School. In addition to those already listed in the text were Charles H. Robinson, Benjamin's son, who went on to become the island's most prolific builder of Victorian-style architecture. Admiral Sir Isaac Coffin Lancasterian School Account Book, 1846–1873, NHA, Coll. 326, Fold. 12.

33. Henry Barnard, *School Architecture; Or Contributions to the Improvement of School-Houses in the United States* (New York: A. S. Barnes & Co., 1848), 124.

34. Barnard, *School Architecture*, 55.

35. Lancaster, *Nantucket in the Nineteenth Century*, xxi.

36. Judith Downey, "Consequences of California Mania: Nantucket and the Whaling Industry," *Historic Nantucket*, vol. 48, no. 3 (Summer 1999), 25.

37. Starbuck, *The History of Nantucket*, 341.

38. Edouard A. Stackpole, *Rambling Through the Streets and Lanes of Nantucket* (Nantucket, Mass.: The Inquirer and Mirror Press, third edition, 1951), 37.

CHAPTER 4:
ROMANTIC REVIVALS, PAGES 108–129

1. Rev. Elias Nason, *A Gazetteer of the State of Massachusetts* (Boston: B.B. Russell, 1874), 353.

2. F. Sheldon, "Nantucket," *Atlantic Monthly* vol. 17, no. 101 (March 1866), 297.

3. Folger & Rich, *Hand-Book of the Island of*

Nantucket (Nantucket: Folger & Rich, Publishers, 1878), 16.

4. Anonymous, "Nantucket as a Sanitarium," I&M, 5 March 1881.

5. The Victorian period refers to the years from 1837 to 1901, when Queen Victoria reigned in Great Britain.

6. Alma de C. McArdle and Deirdre Bartlett McArdle, *Carpenter Gothic: Nineteenth-Century Ornamented Houses of New England* (New York: Whitney Library of Design and Watson-Guptill Publications, 1978), 17.

7. I am grateful to Dr. Jeffery Howe, Boston College, for this information.

8. First introduced in the 1830s, balloon framing did away with the need for hand-hewn joints and massive timbers of post-and-beam construction. In balloon framing the studs rise uninterrupted from sill to rafter and floor joists are nailed to the studs and are supported by horizontal boards. Easier and less expensive, the method freed house shapes from their traditional plane-walled patterns and allowed for easily constructed irregular wall forms.

9. H.T. Perry, "Nantucket Days," I&M, 24 August 1872.

10. The other two houses were built in 1871 for Mrs. Alice Swain and Captain David Thain of Philadelphia on either side of the Frederick Mitchell brick house (69 Main). Both were later demolished.

11. "Improvement," I&M, 20 April 1872. The house was just a few doors down from her son, Joseph Starbuck (1827–1905), a prominent island businessman who lived in the Greek Revival at 96 Main Street.

12. According to Stackpole family tradition, the doors were carved by James Walter Folger (1851–1918), a Nantucket sign-maker, wood-carver, and painter.

13. See, for example, design number 38, "Marine Villa with Tower" in Calvert Vaux, *Villas and Cottages* (New York: Harper & Brothers Publishers, 1864; Dover Publications edition, 1970), 342–343. And "A House Costing

$8,000" in S. B. Reed, *Village and Country Residences, And How To Build Them* (Orange Judd Company, 1878; Lyons Press edition, 2000), 220–221.

14. The original colors are not known, but early photos do show that the trim was painted a darker, complimentary color, as was the custom in homes of that era. The house has been bright blue since 1965, when it was restored; the color was inspired by the "blue" flag stone sidewalk paving in front of the house.

15. E. K. Rossiter and F. A. Wright, *Authentic Color Schemes for Victorian Houses* (New York: William T. Comstock, 1883; Dover edition, 2001), 5.

16. I&M, 8 June 1878; I&M, 16 May 1885. These are just two of many examples of references to colors.

17. Obituary, Eliza Starbuck Barney, I&M, 23 March 1889.

18. She lived with her husband in the home of her daughter and son-in-law, Sarah and Alanson Swain, in Poughkeepsie, New York. Eliza may have been influenced by such mansions as Irving Cliff, in Irvington, N.Y., built in 1868–69 and notable for its distinctive mansard roof, brackets, and rounded arched windows, similar in style to the Barney home.

19. See "Suburban Residence," designed by Isaac H. Hobbs, *Godey's Lady's Book*, vol. 76, no. 451 (January 1868); reproduced in James L. Garvin, *A Building History of Northern New England* (Hanover, New Hampshire: University Press of New England, 2001), 121.

20. For more biographical information on Eliza Barney see Kate Stout, "Who Was Eliza Starbuck Barney?" *Historic Nantucket*, vol. 47, no. 1 (Winter 1998), 10–12.

21. David Bittermann, "The Victorianization of Siasconset: A Discussion of its Late 19th Century Growth," typescript report for Preservation Institute: Nantucket, Summer 1977.

22. See photographs in the NHA's collection of the Ocean View House complex and first dwellings of Sunset Heights.

23. "Town and County," I&M, 30 July 1887; "Valuable Real Estate for Sale," I&M, 15 October 1898.

24. The lot and house first appears in the town deeds books as being sold by Charles H. Robinson to Isabella M. Coffin, October 1886, Deeds Book 71, 126. The ownership of the property after that was: October 10, 1901, to Allen Coffin; August 1906 to Vida C. Sidney; August 1921 to Helen Stowe Penrose; January 1950 to Clement A. and Mary Louise Penrose.

25. The shingle facade now on Wolf's Head was added later. For examples of Sunset Heights cottages see the NHA's photograph collection.

26. For examples of these cottages see Ellen Weiss, *City in the Woods: The Life and Design of an American Camp Meeting on Martha's Vineyard* (Boston: Northeastern University Press, 1987; 1998 paperback reprint).

27. Andrew Jackson Downing, *Cottage Residences* (1873; New York: Dover Publications, Inc., reprinted in 1981), 13.

28. According to the current owner of the house, Mrs. Clement A. Penrose Jr., the house was moved several times, including from Ocean Avenue in 'Sconset to Cottage Avenue.

29. Clay Lancaster, "Charles H. Robinson, Part II," *Historic Nantucket*, vol. 38, no. 4 (Winter 1990), 54.

30. Hunt purchased the land from John A. Beebe for five hundred dollars and hired Robinson to draw up the plans and build the house. See I&M, 8 December 1877. Hunt's coal business was on Old South Wharf. See I&M, 5 October 1878. Hunt sold his house on Broad Street to "a party from St. Louis for $4,000" in 1881. See I&M, 27 August 1881.

31. Other important works by Charles Robinson are 13 North Water Street (ca. 1870); Fair Street, his own home; the Surfside Life

Saving Station (1873); and the Old Stone Barn Inn, originally built as a stable in 1890 for R. Gardner Chase.

32. See designs number 23 and 23a in E. C. Hussey, *Hussey's National Cottage Architecture; or, Homes for Every One* (New York: American News Company, 1874; reprinted in 1994, New York: Dover Publications, Inc.).

33. See I&M, December 1877, and January–February 1878. According to the restorers of 51 Fair, Valerie and Richard Norton, there is evidence that wood boards saved from older structures dating to the 1700s were used in some parts of the house.

34. Early photographs of the house in the Nantucket Historical Association's collection show that the house originally also had articulated vergeboards and pendants.

35. By studying remaining trim on the house, shadows of previous woodwork, indentations in the paint surface, old photographs of the house and surrounding neighborhood, and pattern books from the era, Valerie and Richard Norton were able to re-create the decorative details.

36. Anonymous, "Nantucket," a letter to the editor first published in the Washington *Evening Star*, reprinted in the I&M, 6 August 1881.

37. It is entirely possible she was referring to artist Eastman Johnson who lived on the Cliff, where several residents reportedly painted their summer cottages red. Elma Folger to Jennie Sharp, 1 January 1881. NHA Coll. 270, Fold. 42, Sharp Family Papers.

38. Anonymous, "Nantucket," a letter to the editor published in the Providence *Journal* and reprinted in the I&M, 13 August 1881.

39. A.G.W., "Nantucket," a letter to the editor of the Washington *Evening Star* reprinted in I&M, 6 August 1881.

40. The development of Brant Point was first begun by Henry Coleman, Elijah H. Alley, Franklin Ellis, and Frederick S. Raynard. See Clay Lancaster's *Holiday Island* (Nantucket,

Mass.: Nantucket Historical Association, 1993), 65.

41. *Middletown, Connecticut City Directory, 1877–78* (Hartford, Conn.: Fitzgerald, Dillon, & Co., Publishers & Printers, 1878), 53.

42. The house was enlarged sometime before 1911 and was moved two hundred feet closer to the water in 1975 by owner J. Seward Johnson. For a complete study of the house see Susan Tate and Jay White's "Sandanwede: Nineteenth Century Resort Architecture," unpublished typescript, Summer 1973, University of Florida, Preservation Institute: Nantucket, NHA.

43. Virginia and Lee McAlester, *A Field Guide to American Houses* (New York: Alfred A. Knopf, 1986), 268.

44. I&M, 18 June 1881.

45. See Eugene C. Gardner's *Illustrated Homes: Real Houses and Real People* (Boston: James R. Osgood and Company, 1875) and Henry Hudson Holly's *Modern Dwellings in Town and Country* (New York: Harper & Brothers, Publishers, 1878).

46. Charles Eastlake's 1868 book *Hints on Household Taste in Furniture, Upholstery and Other Details* was extremely influential in the U.S. and spread what became known as the Eastlake style.

47. Obituary, I&M, 14 November 1908. Among Gibbs's other projects: the schoolhouse in Polpis in 1881, and the "New Springfield" Hotel on North Water Street, 1883.

48. Anonymous, "Building Notes," I&M, 28 May 1881.

49. I&M, 18 June 1881.

50. For example, in 1886 the newspaper reported "E. J. Hulbert, Esq., has returned from Europe, and is here for the season." See I&M, 26 June 1886.

51. It was built from plans drawn up by George H. Hammond. I&M, 20 September 1883.

52. Elma Folger to Jennie Sharp, 24 November 1882. NHA Coll. 270, Fold. 42, Sharp Family Papers. Later in the same letter she wrote: "The house, after all, wasn't on Shimmo

Hills—it's way down on Abrams Point—It belongs to a Mrs. Vanderhill—daughter of Charles Dana—Editor of the *New York Sun*."

53. Evelyn T. Underhill, *The Credible Chronicles of the Patchwork Village: 'Sconset by the Sea* (New York: Evelyn T. Underhill & Co., 1886), 22.

54. Advertisement for Almon T. Mowry realtors, I&M, 14 May 1887.

55. According to the Detroit Public Library's records, Rice is listed in the Detroit directories as a bookkeeper in 1866–67 and in the 1870s was the secretary-treasurer of the Detroit Safe Company. He boarded in Detroit at 925 Woodward. His name disappears from the records in 1886.

56. In 1883 Flagg purchased a large tract of land with ocean frontage, stretching south from Sankaty Head Lighthouse, and subdivided a set of lots adjacent to the cliff. See Bittermann, "The Victorianization of 'Sconset," p. 31.

57. The house is situated on three lots; an early photograph shows that at one time there was another house on the lot to the right of Idlemoor, which is no longer there. The photograph also shows that the house originally had an additional top story with a roofwalk. I am grateful to Martha Davis Kelly for this information.

58. In the "Here and There" column, I&M, 29 March 1884, it notes that "E. A. and M. E. Leighton, of Cottage City, are fitting up the new drug store of Dr. James Ginn." Elsewhere M. Leighton's initial is listed as "L." Among M. Leighton's other projects on Nantucket: a cottage on Liberty Street; a billiard and pool hall in 'Sconset; and moving the Surfside train depot building to the 'Sconset terminus. See I&M, June–August 1885.

59. I&M, 15 November 1884.

60. I&M, 25 April 1885.

61. I&M, 23 May 1885.

62. Many thanks to Martha Davis Kelly, who currently owns the house along with Bruce

Davis, for sharing this and other bits of information relating to her family's home.

63. Palliser, Palliser & Co., *Palliser's American Cottage Homes* (Bridgeport, Conn.: Palliser, Palliser & Co., Architects, 1878).

64. The Stick style grew out of the Picturesque Gothic ideals of Andrew J. Downing and flourished in house pattern books in America in the 1860s and 1870s. It reached its height of popularity in the early 1880s.

65. Early photographs of summer houses along the bluff in the 1880s and 1890s indicate that ornamental shingle patterns were a common decorative feature. For example, see photos in the NHA's collection of Flaggship and the Furness Cottage.

66. According to Elinor Vaughter, the house was originally called Heathcliff. It was later renamed Mayflower after "May" Wilson's death in 1899.

67. Their parents were James Ormond Wilson and Sarah Ann Hungerford Wilson; and they had three other sisters: Frances, Anne, and Elinor. The Wilson family stayed at either Castle Bandbox or Heart's Ease, both old whale houses that were renovated into summer cottages. I am grateful to Elinor Vaughter, granddaughter of Elinor Wilson and grandniece of Mary Wilson, for sharing the Wilson family history with me.

68. Garvin, *A Building History of Northern New England*, 126–127.

69. For more biographical information see Obituary, I&M, 3 June 1905.

70. He advertised his lumber business in the I&M; it was located at the head of Old South Wharf in the 1870s and by 1884 was on Whale Street. Among the woods he sold were spruce, yellow pine, oak, ash, black walnut, and white wood.

71. According to current owner of the 76 Main Street Inn, David Cantrell, there is evidence of three levels of expertise in the craftsmanship of the woodwork, indicating that there was a master craftsman and at least two apprentices.

72. As discussed previously, Eastlake's style spread in this country through his popular book *Hints on Household Taste in Furniture, Upholstery & Other Details* (1878; Dover Publications, Inc. reprint edition, 1969).

73. There are other examples of curved brick fireplaces in houses on the island, including one in the Mayflower in 'Sconset, which was also constructed in the early 1890s.

74. The I&M noted on July 4, 1885, "H. H. Richardson, the architect, will occupy the George F. Hammond cottage on Brant Point during the season."

75. "Here and There," I&M, 29 April 1899.

CHAPTER 5:
FISHERMEN'S SHANTIES TO VACATION COTTAGES, PAGES 130–159

1. For more information on the Wampanoags and seventeenth-century whaling see Nathaniel Philbrick, *Abram's Eyes: The Native American Legacy of Nantucket Island* (Nantucket, Mass.: Mill Hill Press, 1998), 62–64.

2. Chester Street (now West Chester) is said to be the oldest road on Nantucket. It led from old Sherburne to Siasconset and was derived from a Wampanoag trail.

3. Many Nantucket anecdotes are based on stories handed down through generations, such is the case regarding the early paths and the note relating the ocean to a stew pond, sited in Henry C. Forman's *Early Nantucket and its Whale Houses* (Nantucket, Mass.: Mill Hill Press, reprint 1991), 12, 34.

4. Forman thoroughly explored 'Sconset's seventeenth-century dwellings in his book, *Early Nantucket and its Whale Houses*. The author is indebted to his book for the guidance it has provided. The early Sesachacha and Siasconset stations are noted on pages 33–34.

5. Forman, *Early Nantucket*, 33. The movement from Sesachacha is also noted in the many HABS reports on Siasconset.

6. The roofs of the houses in old Sherburne were at an angle of approximately fifty-two degrees to the horizon; that of Siasconset was only thirty-five degrees. Forman, *Early Nantucket*, 103. The low height was appropriate for the windy bluff where the whale houses are located.

7. Forman, *Early Nantucket*, 84.

8. Usually attached to the north end of the house, the cooking shed area was called a porch because it was open to the weather. So familiar was the term porch, used for kitchen, that it remained in the vocabulary of both Siasconset and Nantucket town residents for many generations. See Forman, *Early Nantucket*, 96, and Anderson, *Through the Hawse-Hole: The True Story of a Whaling Captain* (New York: MacMillan Company, 1932), 175.

9. Macy Family Papers, 1729–1959, NHA, Coll. 96, Journal 5. For information on wooden chimneys, see Forman, *Early Nantucket*, 97, 112–113.

10. Forman, *Early Nantucket*, 103.

11. Edward F. Underhill, *The Old Houses on 'Sconset Bank: The First History of Siasconset, Nantucket Island, America's Most Unique Village*, ed. by Henry C. Forman (Nantucket, Mass.: Myacomet Press, reprint, 1961), 7.

12. Underhill, *The Old Houses on 'Sconset Bank*, 13–14.

13. "Shanunga (Betsey Cary Cottage)," HABS, Mass-610, 10-SCON 1.

14. Underhill, *The Old Houses on 'Sconset Bank*, 25. In 1872, an official government post office was formerly recognized. Baxter and his daughter were paid employees of the government at approximately eight dollars and twelve dollars per year, respectively.

15. Speculation on the mail slot was discussed with the present owner in a conversation with the late Edouard Stackpole, a highly regarded Nantucket historian. The author thanks Michael Darling for the anecdotal information on Shanunga.

16. Forman, *Early Nantucket*, 4.

17. Nantucket's Historic District Commission published guidelines suggest regulations for home building and renovation. See Kate Stout and J. Christopher Lang, *Building with Nantucket in Mind* (Nantucket, Mass.: Historic District Commission, 1992).

18. Underhill, *The Old Houses on Sconset Bank*, 6.

19. R. B. Hussey, *Nantucket in a Nutshell* (Nantucket, Mass.: Inquirer and Mirror Steam Press, 1889), 30.

20. "Micah Coffin House, Auld Lang Syne or the Captain Henry Coleman House," HABS 857, 10-SCON 2.

21. Forman, *Early Nantucket*, 126.

22. During meetings of Nantucket's Historic District Commission board in 1999, there was a debate as to how far to allow modernization while at the same time protecting the historic integrity of the house. Holly Corkish, "The Two Oldest Houses on Nantucket Island: Siasconset's Auld Lang Syne and Shanunga," typescript report for the Nantucket Preservation Trust, 1999.

23. "Hearts Ease," typescript report for the Preservation Institute: Nantucket, Summer 1983, ref. 90.

24. Forman, *Early Nantucket*, 208.

25. Hugging the bluff, Front Street was not originally the first parallel to the ocean. Erosion caused the loss of a significant portion of beach in an area known as Codfish Park. Still a problem today, erosion of the 'Sconset bluff threatens many homes along the shore.

26. Sited in Forman, *Early Nantucket*, 39–40.

27. Macy Family Papers, 1729–1959, NHA, Coll. 96, Journal 5.

28. The pillars and balustrade are features that indicate that the house may have been a Federal-style design—a style known for it elegant details. Crosby Family Papers, 1812–1893, NHA, Coll. 4, Fold. 2.

29. Florence Bennett Anderson, *Through the Hawse-Hole*, 177.

30. Frederick W. Mitchell sold "the land and dwelling house and other buildings thereon standing" to Eunice Hadwen "to her sole and separate use, free from the interference or control of her husband the said William Hadwen." Book 36, page 169, Nantucket Registry of Deeds, Nantucket Town Building.

31. I&M, 11 August 1877.

32. Ibid.

33. Edward F. Underhill, *'Sconset by the Sea* (Nantucket, Mass.: Underhill, 1887).

34. Edward F. Underhill, *The Old Houses on 'Sconset Bank*.

35. Edward F. Underhill, *'Sconset in a Nutshell* (Nantucket, Mass.: Underhill, ca. 1886).

36. Evelyn T. Underhill, *A Pictyure Booke of ye Pachworke Vyllage Sconsett by ye Sea Ye Pictyures was drawn from others made by Master Wyere and Master Platte by ye Helpe of ye Sunn* (New York: E. T. Underhill & Co., 1886).

37. Evelyn Underhill, *The Credible Chronicles of The Patchwork Village, 'Sconset by the Sea* (New York: Evelyn T. Underhill & Co., 1886).

38. "Siasconset Items," *Nantucket Journal*, 4 August 1887.

39. *Nantucket Journal*, 14 July 1887.

40. I&M, 25 June 1898.

41. See Chapter 4 on Nantucket's Romantic architecture.

42. Archival photographs reveal the chapel's early style. See NHA's Photograph Collection.

43. Purchasing land throughout the 1870s, Flagg eventually owned the entire North Bluff. In 1883, he plotted out eight-five lots, called the section "Sankaty Heights" and began selling the subdivisions. Flagg property included the "Bluff Walk," a land easement given to the town to maintain a ocean-view path for the public.

44. Underhill, *The Old Houses on 'Sconset Bank*, 17.

45. For date of construction, see Amy Jenness, "William Flagg and his Flaggship," *Nantucket Magazine*, vol. 12, no. 1 (Spring 2000), 12–20.

46. While restoring the nineteenth-century exterior sheathing and removing the addition, the interior was given necessary modernization. As a result, some of the original interior features were not retained.

47. Forman, *Early Nantucket*, 207, 220.

48. During an Historic District Committee meeting in 1999, a member is quoted as saying that anything built before 1846 is not "worth the nails holding it together." Corkish, "The Two Oldest Houses on Nantucket Island."

49. Nantucket Registry of Deeds, Nantucket Town Building

50. Reconfigurations are noted on the Sanborn Insurance Company maps on microfilm at the NHA.

51. For more information on Nantucket's Shingle-style houses see Chapter 4.

52. The HDC process was discussed in an interview with architect, David Bentley, who was hired to restore the dormer. The author thanks Mr. Bentley for his guidance and expertise in evaluating the architecture of 'Sconset.

53. Built in 1837, 20 Main Street was mentioned previously in this chapter when it was the vacation home (1855) of Eunice Hadwen.

54. Sanborn maps and historic photographs of the home depict the additions and reconfigurations. See the NHA's photograph collection.

55. The cottages were built on land in the Sunset Heights development first plotted in 1873. Some of cottages appear on the Sanborn maps in 1898. Therefore, the cottages were built sometime between those dates.

56. The property on which the present main building of the Summer House stands was purchased in 1901 by Caroline Parker Hills. According to the 1909 Sanborn maps no houses appear. In 1912, Hills sold the property, and the deed transaction notes that "the tract of land with the building thereon" was sold to Frederick Hall. The building there-

fore was erected between 1909–12. Further research is needed to determine exactly when cottages to the north of the Summer House building were incorporated into the inn.

57. Sometime after 1939, two cottage units were joined together with a section added between the two. The reconfigurations are noted in the Sanborn maps and the deed survey of 1980 located at Nantucket's Registry of Deeds, Nantucket Town Building.

58. Information obtained in an interview with John Shea. The author thanks Mr. Shea for his help in researching his home.

59. Shea purchased the cottages in 1979. He and MacLeod were married in 2000. Since that time, MacLeod has been responsible for the interior design and restoration.

CHAPTER 6: BUNGALOWS, PAGES 160–177

1. L. D. Thomson, "The Rampant Craze for the Bungle-Oh," *Country Life in America* (July 15, 1912), 20.

2. Paul Duchscherer, *The Bungalow: America's Arts and Crafts Home* (New York: Penguin Studio, 1995), 13.

3. "Nantucket Is to Blow its Horn," from the *Brockton Enterprise*, reprinted in the I&M, 1 March 1924.

4. The Radford Architectural Company, *Radford's Artistic Bungalows: Unique Collection of 208 Designs, Best Modern Ideas in Bungalow Architecture* (Chicago: Radford Architectural Company, 1908), 3.

5. The word *bungalow* is from the Hindi word *bangla*, or house in the Bengal style, referring to a type of colonial dwelling in East India. In the early twentieth century, the American Arts and Crafts movement adopted it as the ideal Craftsman-style house. See Alan Weissman, "Introduction," in the reprint of articles from Gustav Stickley's *The Craftsman*, published in *Craftsman Bungalows: 59 Homes from "The Craftsman"* (New York: Dover Publications, Inc., 1988), vi.

6. The number is based on the research of Mark Avery, Nantucket architectural designer, and longtime member of the Historic District Commission. For additional examples of bungalows, not discussed in this chapter, see 4 Charter Street, 20 Milk Street, 2 North Liberty Street; near Brant Point: 3 Walsh Lane, 84 Easton Street; in 'Sconset: 31 Low Beach.

7. Gustav Stickley, "How to Build a Bungalow," first printed in *The Craftsman* (December 1903) and reprinted in *Craftsman Bungalows: 59 Homes from "The Craftsman"* (New York: Dover Publications, Inc., 1988), 1.

8. "'Sconset Notes," I&M, 27 March 1915.

9. "Here and There," I&M, 16 October 1915.

10. "Here and There," I&M, 20 March 1915.

11. The 1914 Nantucket directory lists Quigley as a mason and architect working with William W. Forrester as "Forrester & Quigley," 3 Plumb Lane.

12. Deeds Book 91, p. 350, Nantucket Town Building: Quigley sold the land and house while it was still being built. It is possible that Dr. Grouard purchased the house to be near the island's new hospital that was built a few blocks away on West Chester Street in 1914. However, the 1914 and 1919 Nantucket directories list him as living on Easton. Grouard moved to the island in 1891 and was a family physician for thirty-six years. For more information see his obituary, I&M, 4 June 1927.

13. According to Mark Avery, in the 1920s there were about a dozen stucco houses on the island, many were later shingled over. Examples still existing today in Siasconset: 15 Baxter Road, built ca. 1916, and a Mediterranean Revival-style house on Low Beach Road.

14. His business and home were at 1 Twin Street. He also served as the chief of the fire department. For more information see his obituary, I&M, 1 January 1944.

15. Within a few minutes walk are the Oldest House, 1686, on Sunset Hill Lane, and the Richard Gardner House, 1722–24, at 32 West Chester Street. Formerly called West Centre Street, West Chester is considered to be the oldest road on the island.

16. Another house with hints of the Prairie Style can be seen at 59 Baxter Road, a shingled home featuring a broad, low-hipped roof. Thanks to Mark Avery for this information.

17. Henry Greene (1870–1854) and Charles Greene (1868–1957) are credited with executing the "ultimate bungalows"—exquisitely crafted and designed buildings in the Arts and Crafts style.

18. I am grateful to Mark Avery for leading me to the source that discusses the Greene's time on Nantucket, on breaks from their studies in the Massachusetts Institute of Technology's architecture program in Boston. See Randell L. Makinson, *Greene & Greene: Architecture As A Fine Art* (Santa Barbara, Calif.: Peregrine Smith, Inc., 1977), 28, 30.

19. These battens would generally have been unpainted and stained a rich dark color in contrast to a lighter wall color. In the Nantucket bungalows studied for this book the battens are now painted white and match the wall color, losing this effect.

20. Paul Duchscherer, *The Bungalow: America's Arts and Crafts Home* (New York: Penguin Studio, 1995), 23.

21. Similar to an "inglenook," this type of feature is derived from the English Arts and Crafts style.

22. In 1907 the town voted to allocate a thousand dollars on advertising the island as the "best health resort on the New England coast." See I&M, 23 February 1907.

23. Among the distinguishing features of the furniture and other objects of this style are: hand-finishing, natural materials, and designs that featured sturdy-looking structural elements for visual interest.

24. "Nantucket Captured," I&M, 29 September 1923.

25. Scott Erbes, "Manufacturing and Marketing

the American Bungalow: The Aladdin Company, 1906–20," *The American Home: Material Culture, Domestic Space, and Family Life* (Winterthur, Del.: Henry Francis du Pont Winterthur Museum, 1998), 45.

26. I&M, 8 September 1923; I&M, 19 May 1928; I&M, 11 April 1914; I&M, 16 June 1928.

27. Some island companies sold plans and specifications for bungalows, as well, including William T. Swain & Co. See I&M, 29 June 1912.

28. The homes were made by R. L. Kenyon Co. in Waukesha, Wisconsin, and the on-island agent was Allen Smith. One advertisement touts their homes as "Cheaper than Building," and another says, "You couldn't build a hen house for the money that buys a Kenyon House...." See the "Here and There" column and ad section of these issues of the I&M: 25 May 1912; 1 June 1912; 22 June 1912; 29 June 1912.

29. Many thanks to Mark Avery for pointing out this house to me. See *Radford's Artistic Bungalows: Unique Collection of 208 Designs, Best Modern Ideas in Bungalow Architecture* (New York: Radford Architectural Company, 1908), p. 64.

30. The catalogue offered blueprints for this house with specifications for twelve dollars and the total cost of building was estimated at $2,700–$2,900.

31. I&M, 4 April 1914.

32. See Lancaster, *The American Bungalow: 1880–1930* (New York: Dover Publications, Inc., 1985), 192–193.

33. "Protest Against 'Invasion' of Nantucket Architecture," I&M, 12 September 1925.

34. Hermann Hagedorn, "A Real Problem for Nantucket: The Bungalow Bug," I&M, 3 October 1925.

35. Ibid.

36. Ibid.

37. Edith Correira Perry (1907–1992) was born on Martha's Vineyard, the daughter of Cape Verdean parents, and worked as a cook for the Roberts House and as a nurse's aide at Our Island Home. See obituary, I&M, 13 February 1992. Joseph F. Perry (1899–1961) was born on the island of Fogo, Cape Verde. Thanks to Fran Karttunen for sharing the Joseph Perry information.

38. The Selectmen of Nantucket overturned the Nantucket Historic District Commission's decision to demand the bungalow be retained in its original site. The owners have generously offered to donate the house for affordable housing, and at press time the house was slated to be moved to the Surfside area to be used for low-cost housing. The Selectmen's decision is being appealed in the Superior Court.

39. The term "trophy house" is now a part of the everyday lexicon of Nantucket Island. Mark Voigt, current administrator of the Nantucket Historic District Commission, defines a trophy house as "basically any house that calls attention to itself through its design and location on a lot.... There are many who love Nantucket for its reputation as a prestigious summer resort and therefore want to make their mark by adding another 'trophy' to their usually already bulging portfolio."

CHAPTER 7:
TWENTIETH-CENTURY DESIGN, PAGES 178–189

1. Vincent Scully Jr., *Modern Architecture: The Architecture of Democracy* (New York: George Braziller, 1961, revised edition, 1975), 61.

2. J. Christopher Lang, *Building With Nantucket in Mind: Guidelines for Protecting the Historic Architecture and Landscape of Nantucket Island.* (Nantucket, Mass.: Nantucket Historic District Commission, 1978).

3. The Nantucket Historic District commission is one of only two elected commissions in the country.

4. Brendan Gill, "A Nantucket Tale: An Architect's Family Compound Restates Island Traditions," *Architectural Digest* (December 1999), 159.

5. Gill, 156.

Selected Bibliography

UNPUBLISHED MATERIAL

Blue Files, general subject-indexed files held at the Nantucket Historical Association's Research Library.

Bitterman, David. *The Victorianization of Siasconset: A Discussion of Its Late 19th Century Growth*. A typescript paper for the Preservation Institute: Nantucket, Summer 1977.

BOOKS AND PAMPHLETS

Anderson, Florence Bennett. *Through the Hawse-Hole: The True Story of a Nantucket Whaling Captain*. New York: MacMillan Company, 1932.

Brown, Dona. *Inventing New England: Regional Tourism in the Nineteenth Century*. Washington, D.C.: Smithsonian Institution Press, 1995.

Brunskill, R. W. *Traditional Buildings of Britain: An Introduction to Vernacular Architecture*, second edition. London: Cassell Group Wellington House, 1997.

Calvit, Elizabeth. *The Evolution of Siasconset—From Fishing Village to Resort*. A typescript paper for the Graduate School of Arts and Sciences, Lousiana State University, Baton Rouge, Louisiana, 1991.

Crosby, Everett U. *95% Perfect: The Older Residences at Nantucket*. Nantucket, Mass.: Everett U. Crosby, 1937.

———. *Our Gold Mine: The Dollars Value of the Remaining Oldness of Nantucket Town*. Nantucket, Mass.: Tetaukimmo Press, 1951.

Cummings, Abbott Lowell. *The Framed Houses of Massachusetts Bay 1625–1725*. Cambridge, Mass., and London: Belknap Press of Harvard University Press, 1979.

Douglas-Lithgow, R. A. *Nantucket: A History*. New York: G. P. Putnam's Sons, 1914.

Duchscherer, Paul. *The Bungalow: America's Arts and Crafts Home*. New York: Penguin Studio, 1995.

Duprey, Kenneth. *Old Houses on Nantucket*. New York: Architectural Book Publishing Co., Inc., 1959.

Eastlake, Charles L. *Hints on Household Taste in Furniture, Upholstery and Other Details*. London: Longmans, Green and Company, 1878; reprint, New York: Dover Publications, Inc., 1969.

Forman, Henry Chandlee. *Early Nantucket and Its Whale Houses*, second edition. Nantucket, Mass.: Mill Hill Press, 1991.

Fowlkes, George Allen. *A Mirror of Nantucket: An Architectural History of The Island, 1686–1850*. Plainfield, N.J.: Press of Interstate, 1959.

Gardner, William E. *Three Bricks for Three Brothers: The Story of the Nantucket Whale-Oil Merchant Joseph Starbuck*. Cambridge, Mass.: Riverside Press, 1945.

Garland, Catherine A. *Nantucket Journeys: Exploring the Island, Its Architecture, and Its Past*. Camden, Maine: Down East Books, 1988.

Holly, Henry Hudson. *Modern Dwellings In Town And Country*. New York: Harper & Brothers, Publishers, 1878.

Lancaster, Clay. *The American Bungalow, 1880–1930*. New York: Dover Publications, Inc., 1995.

———. *The Architecture of Historic Nantucket*. New York: McGraw-Hill Book Company, 1972.

———. *Holiday Island*. Nantucket, Mass.: Nantucket Historical Association, 1993.

———. *Nantucket in the Nineteenth Century*. New York: Dover Publications, Inc., 1979.

Lang, J. Christopher, and Kate Stout. *Building with Nantucket in Mind*. Nantucket, Mass.: Historic District Commission, 1995.

Leach, Robert J., and Peter Gow. *Quaker Nantucket*. Nantucket, Mass.: Mill Hill Press, 1997.

McAlester, Virginia and Lee. *A Field Guide to American Houses*. New York: Alfred A. Knopf, 1986.

McArdle, Alma de C., and Deirdre Bartlett McArdle. *Carpenter Gothic: 19th-Century Ornamented Houses of New England*. New York: Whitney Library of Design, an imprint of Watson-Guptill Publications, 1978.

Miller, Judith and Martin. *Victorian Style*. London: Mitchell Beazley International Ltd., 1993.

Morrison, Hugh. *Early American Architecture: From the First Colonial Settlements to the National Period*. New York: Oxford University Press, 1952.

Philbrick, Nathaniel. *Away Off Shore: Nantucket Island and Its People, 1602–1890*. Nantucket, Mass.: Mill Hill Press, 1994.

Plante, Ellen M. *The Victorian Home*. Philadelphia: Running Press, 1995.

Roth, Leland M. *Shingle Styles: Innovation and Tradition in American Architecture, 1874 to 1982*. New York: Produced by Norfleet Press, Harry N. Abrams, Inc., Publishers, 1999.

Scully, Vincent. *Architecture: The Natural and the Manmade*. New York: St. Martin's Press, 1991.

———. *Modern Architecture: The Architecture of Democracy*. New York: George Braziller, 1975.

———. *The Shingle Style: Architectural Theory and Design from Richardson to the Origins of Wright*. New Haven, Conn., and London: Yale University Press, 1965.

Stackpole, Edouard A. *Rambling Through the Streets and Lanes of Nantucket*, fourth edition. New Bedford, Mass.: Reynolds-DeWalt Printing, 1969.

Stackpole, Edouard A., and Peter H. Dreyer. *Nantucket in Color: Profiles of America*. New York: Hastings House, 1973.

Underhill, Edward F., edited by Henry C. Forman. *The Old Houses on 'Sconset Bank: The First History of Siasconset, Nantucket Island, America's Most Unique Village*. Nantucket, Mass.: Myacomet Press, reprint, 1961.

Walker, Lester. *American Homes*. New York: Black Dog & Leventhal Publishers, 1996.

Whiffen, Marcus. *American Architecture Since 1780: A Guide to the Styles*. Cambridge, Mass.: The M.I.T. Press, 1969.

Worth, Henry Barnard. *Nantucket Lands and Land Owners*. Bowie, Md.: Heritage Books, Inc., facsimile reprint, 1992.

Acknowledgments

WHAT began as a project among three women, with strong ties to Nantucket and a passion for the island's architecture, eventually turned into a community-wide project, and as a result we have an enormous number of people to thank.

We owe a special debt of gratitude to Jordi Cabré, for his extraordinary and beautiful photographs, his kind support of our project, and for putting up with unreasonable requests—like taking photographs in unheated buildings on the coldest day of the year. The photography would not have been possible without the generous support of Furthermore: a program of the J. M. Kaplan Fund; the Egan Institute of Maritime Studies/Egan Foundation; and the following individuals, to whom we are extremely grateful: Frank Holahan, Richardson T. Merriman, Caroline Ellis, Georgia U. Raysman, and other anonymous donors.

Thanks also to Alexandra Tart, our patient and fearless editor at Rizzoli/Universe; to Sara Stemen for her beautiful design of the book; to Cesar Rubin for his image editing in the manuscript stage and help with illustrations; Richard Valdes for illustrations of floor plans; and Branislav Bogdanovic and Dilek Katgi for their assistance with illustrations.

We are grateful to Graham Gund for writing the foreword, and to our able writers of the vignettes, including Aimee Newell, Curator of Textiles and Fine Arts, Old Sturbridge Village; Niles Parker, Chief Curator, Nantucket Historical Association; Eric Gradoia, Preservation Planner for the Massachusetts Historical Commission; and John James, architect. Also, we owe a huge debt to our "readers" who generously devoted their spare time to looking over chapters: Aimee Newell; David Bentley, architect; Dr. Jeffery Howe, Boston College; Mark Avery, Nantucket architectural designer; J. Edward Hood, Research Historian, Old Sturbridge Village; and Steve Sheppard, Deputy Director, Egan Institute of Maritime Studies.

A huge thank you to everyone at the Nantucket Historical Association (especially Marie "Ralph" Henke, Elizabeth "Libby" Oldham, and Georgen Gilliam), and the Nantucket Atheneum (especially Sharon Buck Carlee) who spent many hours aiding us in the search for archival photographs and historical documents.

We are extremely grateful to all the house owners, who invited us into their homes and shared their lives and stories with us. In particular John Shea and Melissa MacLeod, Jo Zschau, George Kelly, Robert and Norma Burton, Michael Darling, and the Keller family.

Other individuals on Nantucket who contributed to the research and gave us so much support include Mark Voigt, administrator, Historic District Commission; Valerie and Richard Norton, historic preservationists; Betsy Tyler and Virginia Stotz, freelance researchers; and Holly Corkish, college student and research assistant.

We owe a debt of gratitude to the architectural historians who came before us, especially the late Clay Lancaster; their work served as the foundation from which we built our chapters.

Rose Gonnella and Pat Butler send a personal note of thanks to Margaret Moore Booker, whose diligent work, expertise, and patience brought the whole book together.

Last, but not least, we give our heartfelt thanks to our families and friends (especially Martin Booker, Frank Holahan, Conor and Keegan Butler and Dylan James Butler), who got us through the many stressful times. And the employers of our "regular day jobs" for supporting our efforts: Egan Institute of Maritime Studies/Egan Foundation, Nantucket, Massachusetts; Kean University of New Jersey, Department of Design, Visual Communications Program; and Nantucket Preservation Trust, Nantucket, Massachusetts.

Demolition of the 1875 Monument Grocery Building, 106 Main Street, August 2001.

Despite protests of the Nantucket Historic District Commission and concerned individuals, including the three authors of this book, the 1875 Monument Square Grocery building was demolished by its owners in August of 2001. The Italianate facade was saved and is in storage; its ultimate fate is unknown.

Photograph by Frederick G. S. Clow.

Index